0%
FOR THE
MIDDLE CLASS

THE DAWN OF MIDDLE CLASS
ECONOMIC THEORY

RICH FARRIS

0% for the Middle Class

The Dawn of Middle Class Economic Theory

Copyright © 2014 by Rich Farris.

Inquiries should be sent to:
Rich Farris
Rfarc9@gmail.com

Contents

Money is not the *only* motivator.

ZERO

1968

1968 is ground zero.

Middle class America seems to be hanging on by a thread these days. Maybe it always was. Ortega used to say that civilization is a completely unnatural invention, and because it's so unnatural, people simply don't appreciate how delicate and ephemeral it really is. It stands to reason that the middle class is even more a rarity because there are very few countries that truly have one. A majority of the world still exists in relative poverty alongside extreme wealth. There's nothing natural or certain about our precious middle class. If we don't work harder to preserve it, reverting back to the world norm could easily become the more natural result.

If you live in a thriving middle class that means you live in a country that is able to distribute power, education, opportunity, and wealth to a majority of its population. It is the hallmark achievement of civilization, and we have various ways to measure it. One of the tools economists use to evaluate the strength of the middle class is to measure the wealth gap between the rich and poor. A popular model for this is called the Gini Index. In the poorest countries, the wealth is usually horribly tilted toward a tiny minority of the population. In the countries with a strong middle class, these ratios tend to be more balanced and spread out.

In the United States, our middle class grew in strength and size throughout the 20th century, and as it did, the wealth gap continued to decline. The American Gini Index finally reached an all time low in 1968. In that year, the gap between rich and poor reached its narrowest point in the entire history of this country. This is a little known fact, but 1968 stands out as the best distribution of wealth we have ever achieved. The result also produced the most incredible middle class the world has ever known. In many ways, it has never been matched by any country, anywhere, at any time.

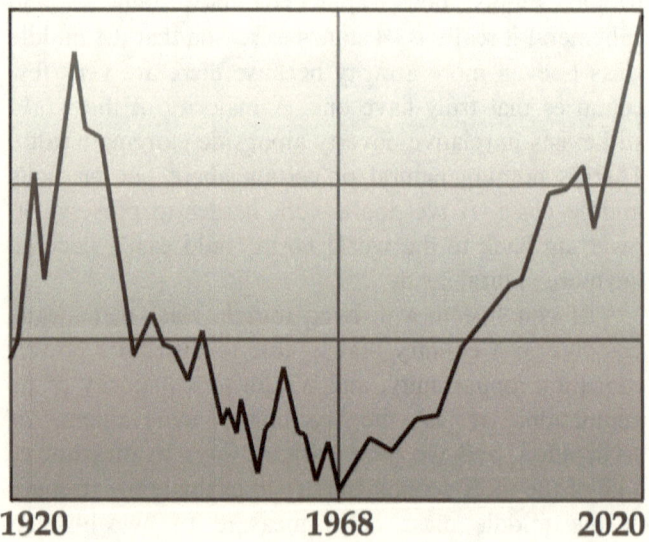

The Incredible Wealth Distribution Peak of 1968

Many well known corporations also peaked in the 1960s alongside our middle class. General Motors was once the largest and most powerful corporation in the world. Most analysts agree that GM reached its peak in the early 1960s before going into a long, slow, steady decline for the following decades. AT&T was next in line, probably reaching its peak in the late 60s. Later, this mighty monopoly was broken up into several parts, allowing several elite participants to make huge amounts of personal wealth from the split. Generally speaking, these giant employers served as excellent representatives of a golden middle class era that bloomed together and faded together, collectively reflecting the strange conditions we see today.

My father worked for AT&T in the 50s and 60s, which provided a nice, warm security blanket for our family. We never had to worry about food, education, or healthcare because my dad's modest job was about as secure as a job could ever be, with ample middle class benefits. It also provided the stability we needed for my mother to start up her own business from scratch, eventually growing it to enough success that my father could take advantage of an early retirement from the telephone company, and join her as a full time business partner.

It's too easy to overglamorize any particular decade. Of course the 60s had its own ongoing problems, including assassinations, racial struggles, and the war draft. But that was also a hallmark decade of liberal progress, where the environmental movement was born. Birth control pills emerged, completely changing the power of women in the workplace. Civil rights finally modernized after a century long wait beyond the Civil War. My father sat on the school board that integrated our schools before I entered the first grade in 1967; therefore, I never actually witnessed segregation. I never saw a segregated restaurant or bathroom, even though I grew up in the South. All of that was quickly expunged before I was old enough to be aware of what it was.

Because I like rock and roll, I would like to give appropriate recognition to our 19th century middle class and working class for inventing it, and taking it to a glorious peak, arguably in 1968. The top song that year was "Hey Jude," the most popular single ever released by the Beatles. For a decade beyond, that was continually voted the best song of all time before eventually fading from cultural memory. The fourth most popular song that year was "(Sittin' On) The Dock of the Bay" by Otis Redding—yet another truly timeless masterpiece that lives on to this day, appropriately reminding us of the average working class man in beautiful, poetic fashion.

Nothing makes the world more promising than the ability to make money, and in terms of pure economics, the middle class was enjoying a time when good pay and reasonable education could be obtained more easily than today. And that seems a bit strange because one would think with each passing decade we would have continued to improve conditions for everybody. Certainly our phones have improved from the days of those old rotary phones. TVs are getting bigger and thinner than ever. The average home size is bigger than it used to be. Cars don't break down as often as they used to. But within this mix of modernizing variables, our financial life has been slowly getting more difficult.

The perks of invention are not enough to hide the insidious problems with the typical middle class checking account.

Nearly half a century has passed by, and fewer Americans are gaining ground the way they used to. Real incomes are not increasing. Employment is not as robust. Education is not as promising or affordable. A lot of people have basically dropped below the middle class. How do we digest this kind of information? Did something go wrong, or was this simply an unavoidable situation that is nobody's fault? What happened prior to 1968 to make the middle class so strong, and what has been happening ever since that continues to weaken it?

Over the past 50 years, our society has become financially corrupt in such subtle ways that the middle class simply sits there in a kind of stupor, not really sure what is happening. Corruption does not necessarily mean anybody is breaking the law. Sometimes the worst kind of corruption is the legalized kind. When those with power cheat, they have ways to make their cheating legal, even if it's not fair. They have advantages that are well beyond what larges masses of others, living more modestly, could ever hope to attain.

It's not in our nature to blame others for our problems. And if you blame all your problems on the rich, they will quickly label you a communist or socialist. The media will help transmit that message loud and clear, to keep you in your place, imposing public shame for daring to question the Monopoly game rules. For nearly half a century, we have been fed a lot of rhetoric that we are expected to accept as proper, proven, free market capitalist economics. But all the while, the middle class keeps sinking, and the richest among us keep getting richer. Where's the *freedom* in free market capitalism if such large groups of people are feeling so imprisoned by the system?

Most economists will admit that life is harder now for the average American than it was for our parents. The middle class math of the 1960s easily trumps the middle class math of the 20-teens. We don't even have an easy way to spell, much less pronounce the current decade we are in, which makes it even harder to properly label our deteriorating situation. The 1960s apparently had superior social mobility. The minimum wage was also higher when honestly adjusted for inflation. This raises the question: Now that the trends have deteriorated to such undeniable proportions, what now? Are things going to get worse? Will our middle class ever again match our 1968 peak?

As you might imagine, the elites are eager to explain that your difficulties have absolutely nothing to do with their excessive success. They will divert the blame to technology, international competition, poor education, immigration, government overregulation, family values, or laziness. They bring a lot of complexity to the table in order to divert you from seeing the uncomplicated facts. Nowhere on their list will you find any mention of their huge, massive wealth playing any role. The most frightening word in the English language for them is *redistribution.* They will battle against this word with all their might, attacking anybody who dares to even look in that general direction.

Our elites will argue that there is nothing harmful about them making incredible amounts of money while the rest of the country struggles to get by. If we try to question too pointedly, they will equate this as an attack on American values. The invisible hand of the marketplace is supposed to allocate assets, money, and resources where it needs to go, and any attempt by us to modify what this *economic Mother Nature* wants to do would be considered both unnatural and unhealthy. That restricts us to the conclusion that it's practically *God's will* that the rich are so filthy rich. Their gains must be interpreted as the result of their hard work and superior intellect, obtained fair and square by the free market system rewarding those who most deserve it, without bias or prejudice.

Were the attitudes different back in 1968? Were the rich getting grouchy and restless back when the American middle class made its unprecedented peak? Maybe they were unhappy to see so many ordinary people doing so well during in a period of fairly progressive taxation. If we look at the numbers it's very obvious that the middle class made an incredible run from the Great Depression to 1968. Then from the 1970s on, the conservative backlash from the elites has successfully taken us all back to something looking more like the Roaring 20s—which was the last known golden age for elite power. When you compare the historic trends between the middle class peak and the wealthy peak, they appear to be opposing forces, like two ends of a magnet.

Around the time our middle class was enjoying its golden 68 victory, the ultra wealthy were indeed getting paranoid that the American system was under attack by communists and socialists within our ranks. There was renewed interest among some of the more insecure elites that the masses needed to be put back under control in order to protect the status quo. While methods for doing this required some planning, this was typically done very quietly, behind closed mansion doors.

Perhaps the most telling moment of the elite backlash could be seen from the public release of a document titled *Confidential Memorandum: Attack on American Free Enterprise System*, authored by Lewis F. Powell, Jr. Shortly before his nomination by President Nixon to the Supreme Court, he wrote a rather detailed report, releasing it on August 23, 1971, to one of the premier corporate elitist organizations in America—the American Chamber of Commerce. He carefully listed a litany of paranoid concerns about college professors, students, and activists possessing dangerous anti-capitalist ideologies. The plan of action he proposed was extremely thorough, espousing the need for corporate power to influence public thought, the media, universities, and text books. This was a plea for other elites to get moving with a more aggressive plan to regain their lost control of the social debate—especially in relation to the teaching of economics. If this memo was any indication, clearly some elites were indeed feeling distraught about the same time that the American middle class had just reached its greatest zenith in the history of civilization. While our parents were sipping down cool ones to Otis Redding and the Beatles, basking in the glory of opportunity never seen in the history of the world, uptight power brokers were scheming in the background over *what went wrong*. Conservative think tanks were forming. Elitist papers were being written. The pendulum was getting ready to swing the other way.

President Reagan was the first sitting President to openly defend elitism and preach the many benefits of letting the rich have as much money as possible. He brought the concept of coddling the rich out into the open as a point of pride. He honed his theory for years, giving his "Little Speech" around the country, until he was able to take it national after finally winning the Presidency in 1981. It was his advisors who helped coin silly phrases like *trickle-down economics*—a term so discredited today, they don't dare use that label anymore. Instead, the terminology has been camouflaged behind a more subtle term known as *supply side economics*. This more aggressive approach to maximizing wealth for those at the top basically bought elites several decades of growth rates to not seen since the Roaring 20s.

For an entire generation, the rich have been on a *tax-cutting-wealth-gap-increasing* rampage. Common sense should easily explain what would happen next. But millions of Americans went along with the fairy tale, imagining that somehow giving more money to the people at the top would magically help the rest of us by some sort of mysterious financial osmosis. But if we look at overall wealth today, the top 1% of Americans own over one third of the total wealth in the United States. The top 5% of Americans own nearly two thirds of the total US wealth. The top 10% of the population owns 75% of the country. The poorest 80% of all Americans own less than 15% of the country's wealth. An unprecedented American oligarchy is now taking root. Nobody really wanted to believe it until Thomas Piketty finally exposed the math in his recent book "Capital in the Twenty-First Century."

The real wake-up call came in 2008 during the massive international banking crash. The percentage of world GDP owned by the world's few thousand billionaires plummeted from 8% to 4% in a matter of weeks, basically cutting their wealth by nearly 50% world-wide. Either number, before or after, is still mind boggling when you consider how few billionaires exist in the world. But 2008, in many ways, hit them far harder than the rest of us. But thanks to the governments who rushed in with trillions of middle class dollars, we were able to save these poor bastards from this horrible fate, not only restoring their wealth, but sending them on to new all time highs by 2014. Most of them were able to hold on to their car collections and multiple 36,000 square foot mansions without any undo suffering.

When you consider that the richest 400 Americans hold more wealth than 50% of the population, these kinds of ratios tend to run in poor countries dominated by corruption and cronyism. It makes you wonder why our government seems so hell bent on running an economy that constantly rewards the most comfortable people in our society while the rest us appear to be getting less comfortable every year. It says a lot about who we are and what we've become. If the United States continues to emulate the actions one would normally find in a place like Russia, it's only a matter of time before we can truly lower our bar to their level. Russia is well known for both its oligarchy and its tortured middle class. The United States has obviously been taking notes. Many of Russia's economic policies are an oligarch's dream—a flat tax rate, low regulation, plenty of space for government bribery, and high levels of privatization. Our play book is not so different from theirs. Ironically, some high ranking American economists have been advising both governments over the past several decades. Little wonder both are now yielding such similar results.

Is the middle class hurting mostly from the crash? Or are we actually hurting more from having to save incompetents who caused the crash? Clearly, our pain began long before 2008. But the very unusual decisions by our government in the wake of this particular crisis began to look extremely suspicious. When the *99% Occupy Wall Street* movement stepped in to the question the situation, the media jumped in just as quickly to discredit the protestors as lazy enemies of American capitalism. Since the media is owned by billionaires, media employees tend to be reluctant to criticize the billionaire point of view.

The protestors were simply trying to shine a light on the primary core of excessive financial power. But elites don't like to be illuminated. It would be embarrassing for them to acknowledge anything was actually wrong with the status quo. The billions of dollars in bonus checks that are routinely paid out on Wall Street is enough money to fund a small country. That's been going on for a while under the raised eyebrows of society. But once their massive failure required hundreds of billions of dollars from middle class tax coffers, the average American was not supposed to take notice. We were told that the bailouts were actually meant to protect *us* from certain world depression. However, this time the masses began to question who was actually saving whom. We have all been told for years that capitalism was supposed to ruthlessly punish the incompetent by allowing them to fail. Yet, these bailouts did not smell at all like free market capitalism. For once, the preachers of Wall Street were not practicing what they preach. The rules seem to apply to everybody except for those at the very top of the pyramid. Apparently, they got to live by a very different, far more forgiving set of rules.

Elite power doesn't take public skepticism sitting down. A long line of them passed through CNBC studios on a regular basis to blast all the Wall Street protests. Likewise, very few politicians stuck their neck out on this one, lest they not get invited to their next political fund raising dinner. Their bribery checks could get cut off if they were to boldly side with the majority.

Sadly the argument behind the 2008 market crash and the ensuing Wall Street protests got reduced to childhood arguments where you were either for capitalism or against it. There was no middle ground allowed in the discussion. Populism is a scary word among the super rich. They tend equate words like that with the end of civilization. Guarding their wad like some police officer at a crime scene, "Just move on folks, there's nothing to see here."

When you see things that don't make sense you may not always understand why it's happening, but there tends to be an immoral core beneath the suspicion that carries substantial truth to it. Power, in general, warps a lot of minds. Egotosis, richmania, and arrogantitis are very common diseases among the filthy rich. It's a condition that used to only get caught by kings, queens, and dictators, but in today's world, modern American oligarchs are much more susceptible to infection than ever before.

The 2008 crash was a symptom of excessive elitism finally collapsing. This condition was very much related to the ongoing movement of wealth into the hands of the few. And now a part of that excess was actually trying to fail. And whether or not this failure required a bailout, the irony is that none of this ever had to happen in the first place. There were countless ways this highly preferential treatment could have been thwarted in advance. Some economists believe this disproportionate wealth ratio will eventually fix itself in one huge swoop, a bit like it tried to do during the 2008 crash. The problem is, every time the market gods try to straighten out the excess, governments tend to rush in to patch it all back. In summary, most governments are literally desperate to protect their precious billionaires from any harm. In moments like these, we can now see where the real marching orders come from.

The odd thing about economics is that it's a lot like cancer, evolution, or global warming. You can't always see change happening in the short term. It often takes a fair amount of time to realize whether or not you have been screwed by the system. It took people over forty years to realize that the super rich really are taking advantage of the rest of us, even if a reasonable explanation for it has not been forthcoming. When the elites hit their own crisis, of their own making, the evidence came into super clear focus for the entire world to see. That's the point when all the dogma that's been fed to us for so many years finally starts to ring hollow. It's a bit like when true love evaporates from an insult that can't be put back in the bottle. The trust is gone. She simply doesn't love you anymore. The kiss no longer feels right.

The main problem here is one of indoctrination. Per Justice Powell's 1971 recommendation, the elites now have firm control of the conversation *and* the ideology. The belief system that most Americans have been taught regarding economics is basically a billionaire's ideology. While Reagan deserves a lot of credit for finding ways to sell extreme elitism to the average American, the indoctrination goes much further and deeper than that. Our university education system, particularly in the field of economics, is entirely based on the billionaire's perspective.

The major dividing line in economics falls between liberals and conservatives—Keynesians versus the libertarian Austrian School respectively. In political life these systems get roughly translated to Democrat and Republican labels. But both of these systems have been carefully filtered to align with *billionairism*. The conservative-liberal divide is a bit of an illusion. Both of these so called extremes have been carefully crafted to actually fit the same wallet, which is certainly not the middle class wallet. While Democrats and Republicans pretend to be harsh adversaries, they both effectively work for the same employer. When problems fail to be properly repaired, each side will claim the shortcomings only happened because their own dogma was not adhered to with adequate purity.

Middle class life does not function by the extremes of abstract thought. The far left and the far right are not accurate models of reality and never were. When people take abstract concepts to extremes in order to define a solitary truth, there is nothing in reality to ever make it pure and perfect. These extremes are the very things that make life unstable for the country as a whole.

Corrupt elites have nourished this incompetent gridlock of extremes because they need moderate thought to come to a complete standstill in order to benefit from radicalized instability. Granted, it's not unstable from their point of view. An imbalanced flow of power is what they seek to stabilize for their own benefit. But the fact is their theories and their system stand squarely in the way of what is best for a thriving middle class. Anybody who questions this contradiction between the interest of the few versus the interest of the many need only look that the results of the past five decades.

Elites have very cleverly financed a social war that pits middle class conservatives against middle class liberals. It's a convenient art of distraction that keeps the discussion away from any class based analysis. If we are ever going to get the middle class fixed, we are going to need to accept that the conservatives have a few things correct, and the liberals have a few things correct. If we can stop polarizing this reality we can end the nonsense and get things back on track with the vague, gray truth called reality. As long as our middle class remains so divided, there will be no fix. United we stand, divided we fall. We can have an America for the few, or we can have an America. We can have a Mitt Romney America, where the poorest 52% of us are feared and disrespected. Or we can try to have an America that seeks to restore the middle class back to its long lost 1968 gold standard.

If the middle class can ever get the independence of thought to stop worrying about what is liberal and what is conservative, we can finally focus on what is needed to protect and rebuild our damaged financial structure. The infighting over social values is a very effective method of social control. Politicians use infighting style arguments to create meaningless sideshows. It's a convenient type of incompetence that is well known in the majority of the world—the third world—where middle class existence is virtually extinct. Gridlock is the best friend of the corrupt elitist.

What this gets down to is the nature of our belief system that regulates our economic view of the world. We live in a free market capitalist society. That is true, or sort of true. Unfortunately, our government is basically run by very wealthy people with way too much power and control over virtually everything, thus, the explanations we receive for how an economy should be managed is not accurately linked to how it actually *is* managed. If you turn on a business channel like CNBC or Bloomberg, you will get a lot of economic business theory. The person doing the talking might not be super wealthy, but it doesn't matter. What you will hear is basically a highly indoctrinated outlook that virtually all billionaires agree with. These media employees would be humiliated by their peers if they were to ever veer off course from the doctrine. In fact, anybody who dares to sing off key becomes a punch line. The social forces are there before your very eyes, constantly weeding out any critical thought, maintaining a consistent religion that the congregation obediently conforms to. And as this belief system gets more warped and more disjointed from our real world, a tiny little question about competency starts to sneak into the background.

The only way to get past this stalemate is to redefine our economic system, not through a billionaire's distorted vision, but through the eyes of the middle class. We need to describe an economic model based on our broad needs and values, not theirs. That's not as easy to do as you think because their brainwash machine runs at full speed, 24 hours a day. It puts out a lot of noise and goes after anything that challenges it with vicious anger, vengeance, and disdain. The blowback of conservative wealthy power after 1968 was nothing short of a tsunami against the middle class—a massive wave that has yet to subside after nearly five decades.

The establishment does not like to think that their precious system has anything wrong with it. But they have had several decades to sell their ideas to the rest of us, and the time has come to size everything up. They got absolutely everything they wanted. We handed them the keys to the car and they drove it into the ditch. If their ideas were so fantastic and correct, we should all be singing their praises right now, bathing in success together. But 1968 gives us a reference point that is revealed even more clearly today. From our faded current position, it shines back to us like a beacon over stormy waters, with increasing clarity as our boat floats away without an oar. The idea of *progress,* that was taken for granted for so long, suddenly comes into question as we start to feel our collective slide backwards over such an extended period of time.

The economists of the past century have demonstrated that they have no real clue what makes the middle class tick because no economist has ever successfully articulated an economic theory from our point of view. There has never been a true middle class economic theory because nobody ever recognized the magnificent, yet extremely rare, perhaps even lucky existence of a strong middle class in modern society.

Nobody ever took note of the extraordinary milestone achieved in 1968, and the fleeting speed with which it has been hauled away.

If we can agree that a problem exists, we can finally start to look the issue in the eye, instead of glancing around the room like a bashful kid, hoping some group-think process will cure our ills. We need to re-center and recalibrate economic theory to sit squarely over the center of gravity of our 1968 example. The nucleus of a truly functional theory should be designed to reflect what our parents created, not only as an economic accomplishment, but as a maximum measure of civilization itself.

You can liken this effort to developing a champion basketball team. In basketball, the best team is not necessarily the team with the best player. If one player scores most of the team's points by himself, that would be comparable to an elitist economy. When just a few have all the power, the total group is relatively weak. The best basketball teams are the ones that maximize the power of all five of its players on the court. When power gets distributed to the entire team, suddenly the team begins to function well beyond the individual level. While the media could not stop worshipping the individual power of LeBron James in the 2014 NBA finals, the San Antonio Spurs had something harder to worship—a great *team*. They were less athletic than many of their adversaries, yet superior in how effectively they distributed their power as a unit.

The current American economy is like a team where too many players are sitting on the bench doing nothing. In order to recalibrate, we will need to take a long hard look at money, what is it for, how is it used, and how do people react to it. If there is any desire to protect and rebuild a healthier wealth model, we will need to construct a new theory that is middle class based. The middle class is a team, whereas the elites live in a world of individual idol worship. Our new acronym will be referred to as *MC Economics* (Middle Class Economics), designed to both challenge and replace the failed belief system currently in play today. In order to break with outdated indoctrination, we will have to identify key pieces of the old religion that are defective, so we can replace it with opposite approaches that will operate with better intention.

Thought usually precedes action. Until we clear up the thought, the action will continue to flounder around incompetently, rewarding the wrong recipients for the wrong reasons. Elites have been carefully constructing their own model for many years, slowly feeding off the vast wealth of our parent's glorious accomplishment. It is because of our collective wealth that elites have been able to elevate their own personal wealth into the stratosphere. But their excess is clearly weakening the whole body. What they did for themselves can easily be rewired to do plenty more for the rest of us. It sounds like common sense, but these days, common sense has been in very short supply. The battle for wealth and power begins with the battle of ideas, and we have some intellectual fighting to do against an adversary that has never been more powerful than now. So let's get started.

MC: Middle Class Economic Theory

The Cost: Economists will scoff at the potential gains projected for the middle class in this book using *MC Theory*. But that's only because none of them have ever tried to reimagine what we would truly be capable of if we only had the opportunity to live under a middle class centric economy. 1968 gave us a glance at the possibilities, but this country has yet to get serious about exploring what kinds of peaks we could really achieve as a unit. Our only limitation is the permission to succeed. The middle class needs its freedom. It is sad that we are held back by something so easy to fix; yet, that should also give us hope that it is so easy to fix.

The only person who cannot imagine a free world is the slave owner.

ONE

Moralnomics

Economics is not a math problem.
It's a moral problem.

The thought process we use to deal with various problems makes little shifts and changes from generation to generation. They way we see the world is a little different than how our parents saw it. The way our grandparents saw the world was different than how our great grandparents saw it, and so on. Each generation moves through the world like caravan, dealing with a unique set of problems, and thus, altering priorities on how to think. These little modifications to our point of view define who we are as a generation.

Over the past several centuries, the changes to our world and how we see it have been massive to say the least. Over the long term, it gets to be impossible to visualize the world the way it was seen by distant ancestors. For example, the Greeks and Romans had no science to aid their thought process, so they were forced to view their entire environment through a highly metaphorical lens. *Everything* they saw, they saw metaphorically. The context of their thinking was so radically different from ours, it's virtually impossible to put our mind in their shoes.

The transition from the ancient mindset to the Enlightenment was an enormous intellectual evolution built on scientific reasoning slowly replacing metaphors, one by one, bit by bit. The United States was very lucky to have been founded in the late 1700s because we were essentially "imagined" during the very last chapter of the pre-modern era—where reasoning was making its first full transition into logical, secular scientific justification. While religion struggled with justice and governance for thousands of years with only basic, moral tools to work with, the secular world of reasoning was taking over moral judgment, separating everything into novel bits and pieces.

Virtually all of the social sciences did not exist as an academic discipline until the 1800s. As these new categories of thought took on greater definition, it was believed that the social sciences were also scientific. The natural assumption was that virtually all problems of the world would eventually be solved and understood through logic and reasoning. But it didn't take long for skeptics to step in and put that fantasy to rest. Science and social science in fact sit on opposite sides of an enormous intellectual gap. These are two different worlds that operate from completely different foundations. A social science like economics can only *try* to be scientific. It can pretend. But science it is not. The gulf between social science and science is not only permanent and insurmountable, but constant awareness of this disconnect is highly essential. Science lives in a world of proof and replication. Social science lives in a world that must deal with vague, unique conditions under constant change. The bottom line, it's a lot easier for an economist to tell a lie than a scientist.

But modernization played a bit of a cruel trick on our mind. We didn't actually abandon the metaphor as a basis for thought. What really happened was we simply improved our metaphors, making them more specific to the task at hand. We certainly displaced a lot of fiction with fact, as our logic and knowledge improved. But what has been largely misunderstood is the underlying reality that every new discovery to this very day is still highly dependent on our metaphorical skills.

The transition into the Industrial Age, where machinery began to replace human labor, had a radical and lasting effect on our new view of the world. For the first time, our inanimate world started taking on a life of its own. The invention of steam engines, trains, internal combustion engines, bullets, and electricity all happened over just two or three generations. The mechanics of the Industrial Revolution created a very new kind of metaphor for our minds to deal with—the concept of self-regulation.

The emergence of the machine as virtually a living, breathing, inanimate object, has contributed to the objectification of human labor, making machines and humans competing, interchangeable variables in the industrial marketplace. As mechanization replaced human labor as a self-regulating object, suddenly the economic relationship between government and people began to change at a dangerous pace, creating some confusion in the field of economics as well.

One of the unique characteristics of modern, mechanized civilization has been the attempt to create a self-regulating economic system that runs more like a machine than something man made. This has, somewhat accidentally, led to a form of governing that is largely seen as an amoral or non-judgmental tool. Where immorality is the polar opposite of morality, amorality seeks to avoid personal judgment altogether by taking on an increasingly inanimate role. As our machines get more powerful, our environment has been slowly getting more dehumanized.

There are several conveniences to this transition to an amoral foundation. By setting people free to operate exclusively with amoral tools, it frees everybody up to function in an economy where each person can have more control over their own decisions. Self-determination comes into full view when the law no longer tries to judge you in advance as moral-centric mechanism. Amoral systems have made it easier for your birth right, race, and sex to diminish as a limitation. This was certainly not the case in the preceding religious based, highly humanized ruling systems, where social regulation was very strict and highly judgmental.

If we look back at our parents' 1968 miracle, their achievement was not made over a few years. It was literally a lifetime achievement that began with the Great Depression. They were cut from a very different cloth. The amoral transition in their thought process had not reached its full transition in their time. Their distance from the older metaphorical-moral based view of the world was still lingering in the back of their mind as they began to create a more amoral system. This combination gave them some invisible advantages that were completely lost by their children. In other words, their thoughts came from a mixture of both moral judgment and amoral regulation, which became a powerful balance for optimum social decision making.

Moral thought seeks to right a wrong between people. Amorality isn't so much a thought as it is a thing that can be used by whoever touches it. For the purposes of this chapter, both of these core concepts will need to be held in clear view so that we may see how they have been smartly used by the middle class up until 1968, and smartly destroyed by elites leading up to our situation today. The primary failure of modern economics is based on its failure to distinguish between the amoral and the moral.

Contemporary economic theory tries to define the world with impersonal, objective terminology like *supply*, *demand*, *risk*, *productivity*, and *asset allocation*. These are amoral tools that fit well with mathematics. They don't judge activity, they simply calculate it. The assumed human connection, sitting in the shadowy background of these mathematical relationships is only referred to casually under bland, subjective terms like *the pursuit of happiness*, *work ethic*, or *motivation*. The desire to emulate science has put economics on a pretentious foundation of "proof." The amoralization of modern economic theory has basically diminished or possibly even destroyed the critical link to moral judgment.

The failure of modern economics to successfully protect and serve the middle class is proof enough that something is missing from the thought process. Then again, the existence of a *real* middle class is too rare to really be known by common economic theory anyway. Most contemporary economic concepts sit on a foundation born out of the more elitist Gilded Age—an era that actually predates the existence of a true, modern middle class. Elites have been around forever. The middle class is like a newborn baby by comparison.

The middle class, as known from American culture, is a mid-20th century invention. It was born in part from the very recent increase in human health. Since the dawn of civilization, average life spans had trouble getting beyond the age of 28. That was the rough average for thousands of years until the Industrial Age got going with better water and sanitation. The challenges of survival in the pre-modern era largely prevented a true three class system from ever evolving.

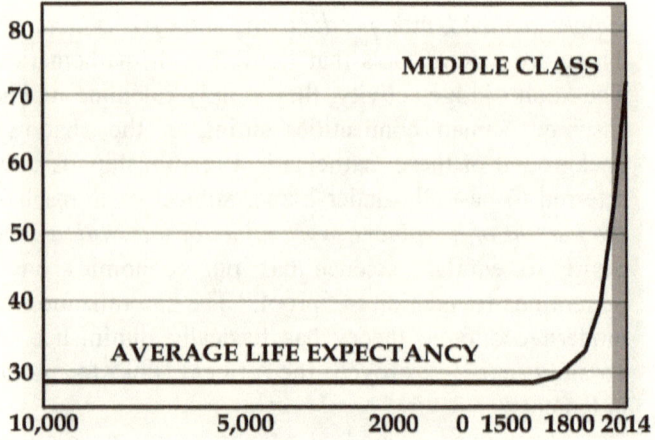

The History of Life Expectancy Relative to the Emergence of the Middle Class

The American middle class peak of 1968, that subsided almost as quickly as it showed up, was seen for the very first time in an age when most people mistook it for modernism, incorrectly focusing on the novelty of our technology, rather than the marvel of our financial morality. Sometimes a new thing can hardly be seen until it finds a contrasting element to point it out. The Beaver Cleaver era brought it to our being in the 1950s, but the Civil Rights Movement probably did the most to bring its definition to our attention because it emphasized that some outsiders were being unfairly excluded from the miracle.

Our new middle class was mischaracterized through a typical elitist interpretation. American military dominance, alongside an emerging Cold War, helped to form the American interpretation around nationalistic explanations for our success. This new ideology dominated as a classless justification, pitting Americans against the world, rather than the middle class versus elites. The externalized nationalistic struggle largely overshadowed the existence of an internal one, with the one pesky exception of lingering racism.

America's financial success of the 20th century, coupled with its hyper-antagonistic competition with communism, helped to split off Karl Marx as a polar opposite to Adam Smith in our intellectual culture. The former served as a kind of antichrist to the Western economic miracle. The unique characteristic of Marx's economic philosophy was that he was the first economist to make class based tension a primary tenet to his economic thesis. American McCarthyism vilified the socialist belief system about as strongly as the Church once vilified Galileo, and thus, an entire body of thought was basically shamed away from American indoctrination for decades to come. Marx was intended to be ignored. Going unnoticed was the fact that even Adam Smith, as far back as the Enlightenment, also took class interests into account, and predicted that the business class could take on too much power and control over the consumer, effectively disabling the system if not kept in check. That part of Smith's work has been conveniently overlooked in favor of his more objective, amoral analysis.

But finding relationships between our situation today and the theoretical work of Marx or Smith is somewhat pointless, given that the world that inspired their ideas has so little in common with modern life. The lifestyle and mechanics of today's world allows for levels of hedonism, free time, survival, and financial accumulation that neither Marx nor Smith would have ever been able to imagine in their far less resourceful era. The generational shifts simply leave too big of a gap to make many worthy connections.

The 1968 middle class peak happened just before the advent of the new electronic era. As the computer reared its head to the financial world, a few thousand elites began to accelerate away from the rest of the world population to levels of wealth that can scarcely be imagined. The electronic age has spawned a computerized market system where assets and power can be transferred in milliseconds around the globe. The fact that a single person is able to gather more money than literally billions of other people combined, is a ratio of accumulation not possible until the advent of electronic banking. Simple market hiccups in the vast financial machinery can cause the instant reallocation of billions of dollars from the many to the few. Not even slavery was able to leverage this kind of power. Never has so little effort been possible to gain so much by so few. Making money from money, rather than from real, actual work, has emerged as a fantastic gift to those few who are best equipped to take advantage. This newfound financial speed presents very new dangers that have not been adequately addressed by policy makers.

Modern economics presumes to advance itself through the use of complex math. The assumption being that this can provide a so called "improved" view of reality, much the same way Stephen Hawking might use difficult equations to explain the age and origin of the universe. Risk and reward converge as concepts to be mathematically rediscovered, like some property of gravity, or the speed of light. The hyper-specialization of today's approach is completely opposite our forefathers' view of economics. Their theories rested on broad generalized views of the world, completely immersed in the moral human condition, whereas the more mathematical economists of today are blinded by their own amoral equations, largely divorced from the actual humanity involved. Specialized education has the evil flaw of making an expert ignorant of almost everything beyond his tiny restricted view of the world. [See Ortega's "The Revolt of the Masses" for a more detailed critique of specialization.]

By making all economic knowledge specialized and narrow, the larger view of what is happening to society gets excluded from the conversation, and therefore excluded from economic analysis. The microscopic amoral world view starts to rule over all key decisions because the macro-moral view has been abandoned as pointless. This plays into the hands of elites who hold a permanent head start to what has essentially been turned into a macroeconomic board game. They play the game with their eyes on the board while the middle class gets to play blind folded. By keeping attention away from the nature of the game, this micro-amoral approach keeps the victims of any fraud blind to the robbery. By taking advantage of the *invisible hand* of market forces—as exploited from the vocabulary of Adam Smith—our elites are able to divert moral judgment away from their massive financial gains. Instead, dry formulas are used to explain the *nature* of markets without giving any thought to the appropriate goal of markets. This has the effect of turning our modern Monopoly game into an assumed reality that is natural and god-given, rather than man-made and changeable. It helps to force people to avoid giving any thought to applying political pressure to intervene because the existing system was conceived to look biologically self-sufficient. Reasoning itself becomes cornered, or worse, completely excluded, as elites try to get us to play along with their robotic world set in motion with presumptuous inertia.

If you look at the share price charts of most major Wall Street banks from 1990 to 2007, you will see a perfect illustration of a massive financial bubble getting ready to pop in the stock market. What is most important to note here is the behavior of those attending this excessive orgy of financial success at that time. The jubilant participants received huge praise for their genius in creative banking. The CEO's of these banks were worshipped like gods by the financial media, with their faces plastered on the covers of magazines and business journals. The major players typically had advanced degrees in finance, business, or economics, mostly from very expensive, prestigious schools. These were highly educated people, highly studied in money, working in the money industry, and getting paid enormous sums of money.

The last thing anybody wanted to see during this meteoric market climb was a party pooper. Anybody who might want to consider criticizing this golden moment would be frowned upon, criticized, or virtually ignored. Our billionaire economic system measures brains with dollars, and as dollars rise, high IQ gets assigned to the highest bidder. The ideology becomes a self-reinforcing form of corporate tribalism.

When the 2008 crash arrived, we now know that many of these banks, mortgage lenders, investment banks, and insurance companies basically collapsed because of their inability to properly control credit default swaps and mortgage backed derivatives. These so called geniuses had created a math model that was very complicated and overly creative, and they were proud of their complex brilliance at the time. This was known as "financial innovation." We should have already known at the time, thanks to Enron's crash in 2001, the only proper place for a *creative* accountant is jail. In 2008, several of our largest and most prestigious financial institutions began to fail, despite their employment of highly educated "experts" in the field of finance. An entire financial industry was basically too ignorant to understand its own financial incompetence.

In the financial media, the problem was equally unimpressive. None of the financial journalists, or virtually none, were reporting any concerns whatsoever about the growing banking bubble prior to the crash. There were a few exceptions, but those smart enough to see this impending disaster were few and far between. Most of the media was caught up in endless idol worship, spurred on by their need to sell ad space. But there is one business journalist who stands out as a major exception. Her name is Gillian Tett. Her story is now well known as one of the few who began to spot a serious problem well in advance of the crash.

She came in late to the party. It wasn't until 2005 that she began to study the banking industry, long after it was already well into the bubble building stage. As she learned the details of what they were doing, she began to be alarmed. She became one of the rare skeptics on Wall Street trying to report a problem during the drunken party of excessive gains and massive bonuses. The geniuses were not paying her much heed as their massive size in the marketplace greatly outweighed her singular voice. Contrarians are rarely appreciated until everybody else is finally proven wrong. If somebody dares to preach for moderation during a period of excess, it is typically rejected as unwarranted Puritanism. We have become a culture that worships excess because we live in a billionaire's world, and nothing spells *too much* more clearly than *billionairism*.

But we have no yet arrived at the important punch line to this story. The fact that Ms. Tett got it right and nearly all of her peers got it wrong is made even more significant by the very fact that she does not even have an education in finance. Most of her peers in the financial media have business degrees—the very same education obtained by the people they report on. But Ms. Tett had something more powerful than an MBA. She holds a PhD in anthropology. How is it possible that an anthropologist turns out to be smarter and more insightful about banking practices than a bank CEO holding an Ivey League MBA?

In Wall Street lingo, Ms. Tett would be what they call a *contrarian*. A contrarian has the ability to think opposite the herd, and this is a somewhat rare skill that few people can pull off. It requires an ability to question authority, and most people are not naturally comfortable doing that. But most effective contrarians, by their very nature, are generalist thinkers who are capable of looking at the big picture. Anthropology is a form of education that provides a big picture view of culture and history. In her book "Fool's Gold" Ms. Tett has thoroughly documented how she was able to decipher the tribal codes and social order of the banking tribe the same way an anthropologist might analyze an ancient culture. And based on her broad knowledge of cultural history, she was trained to see ideology objectively, rather than be consumed by it. While anthropologists may not be experts in money, they *are* experts in ideology, cultural habits and societal weaknesses, which is ultimately what was critical here for getting a clear picture of the problem. A macro-view of any culture is ultimately a moral view because when one is able to think critically at that level, nothing is sacrosanct. It either functions as a whole organism or it doesn't.

The people in charge of our largest banks, the Federal Reserve, and the Treasury Department, are mostly money oriented, money educated people, who don't know anything about our economy as a whole. They are heavily indoctrinated by ideologies that fit the same mold that caused this crash in the first place, and they are the very same people who were brought in to clean up the mess after it broke down. They have no big picture view, even though many of them pour over macroeconomic statistics all the time. Their actions fail at the moral level because they have no ideology in place to govern the integration of moral thought to their amoral tools. In many ways, their job descriptions and ideology most likely discourage macro-moral judgment as unprofessional and unnecessary behavior. Their education is exclusively micro-amoral.

If we want to maximize America's middle class, we are going to need to identify two things right up front before we can go any further. Rule number one is that excessive financial windfalls in our economic system are not healthy for the middle class. Rule number two is that we will need to find the appropriate time and place to apply moral judgment to our objective, regulatory processes. We can never fear intervention when the economic machine starts to yield immoral, imbalanced results. It is paramount that we bring morality back into the economic equation.

In the 1960s, we had a Federal Reserve chairman who seemed to understand the interplay between amoral regulation and moral outcome. His name was William McChesney Martin. He held chairmanship of the Fed from 1951 to 1970. In many ways he was the ultimate guardian of the middle class and probably the greatest Federal Reserve chairman to ever hold that position. He invented the well known phrase *it is my job to remove the punch bowl just as the party gets started*. That famous and often repeated quote says it all because that kind of moral based thought process is conspicuously absent in today's Federal Reserve. McChesney consistently resisted pressure from politicians to loosen monetary supply. He fought against inflation, and he stuck to very modest policy decisions, placing stability above all other priorities. Over time, Presidents who criticized him for not playing ball with their short-term political objectives would continue to reappointment him because his integrity was beyond question. And considering that our 1968 miracle happened on his watch we have to give him some credit. He stood as a balance *against* power, instead of being a lever *for* power—pretty much unheard of in today's government.

Mr. McChesney was basically an elitist himself, but he took on the job of Federal Reserve chairman with great concern for all citizens. He did not believe in a *free for all* economic system that played exclusively by the *rules of the jungle*. Having lived through the Depression he knew all about the dangers of excess, which helped him to prioritize moral decisions that were always in the better interest of the long term over the short. His thought process was more in line with the real Adam Smith, rather than the stripped down amoral version so often quoted by today's ideologues.

If you think about economics in terms of real results, then ask yourself this question: Which person has done the most to affect middle class economics in a positive way over the past generation? Since 1968, times have gotten increasingly difficult for the middle class in general. But in this same span of time, where have we seen the most credible, obvious, middle class success that is real and tangible? Based on middle class reality, we could point to Dr. Martin Luther King, Jr. as the most significant economist of our time. Despite his senseless death in our otherwise celebrated year of 1968, he led a movement that did far more to help deprived members of a poverty stricken group than any economist ever did. The success of his movement seemed hopeless in his day, but the positive results today are quite obvious, opening the doors of the middle class to millions of others. Most importantly, this economic achievement was not based on complex math, but very simple moral principles. There was plenty of amoral analysis standing in his way, trying to prevent success. The only tool his movement could use was the hammer of moral embarrassment. By putting morality front and center, he outweighed the validity of any competing economic theory. Martin Luther King never won a Nobel Prize for economics, but as a successful contrarian to immoral power, he most certainly should have. Economics can only defend the middle class when it prioritizes morality into the equation while resisting unhealthy excess.

MC-1: The middle class must resist economic theories that seek to exclude moral variables. We must return to moral oversight as the primary navigator of our amoral economic processes.

The cost: The current immoral imbalances in our economic system are costing the middle class trillions of dollars. We are effectively living with one arm tied behind our back for no justifiable reason. Our overall wealth and well being should be at least 25% higher than current levels. Any progress will very likely require unrelenting moral embarrassment.

TWO

Recession

The middle class is a 40 year bond.

If we may state the obvious, the middle class is not in charge and actually has very little power over policy in this country. We are large in number, and yes, we do get to vote. But we have a very formidable adversary with far more power and control over the system. They are small in number of votes, yet massive in terms of the votes they can cast with their checkbook. They have figured out countless workarounds to put their needs and desires ahead of yours, and they have been refining these shortcuts for decades. The masses are important only to the extent that their consumer behavior can be mined for corporate wealth. It's assumed to be a two way street, a win-win situation. But the data is quite tilted to one side for those willing to take an honest look at exactly how the game really works.

Billionaires and their international corporate elites run the political donor dinners. The middle class is not invited, although we get to work in the kitchen. Elites not only control the politicians, they also pick and choose all of the critical positions in the bureaucracies. Regulators sit in revolving door jobs with those they are supposed to regulate. It's a form of corporate nepotism that has completely overrun our government.

Actual family based nepotism runs rampant in Congress. There are loopholes where politicians can funnel large sums of money to their spouse, kids, nieces and nephews with pretend political jobs. Not only can they keep their so called elected positions forever, but their entire family gets to go along for the ride. Ironically, one of the worst Congressional offenders of nepotism, according to *60 Minutes,* has been Ron and Rand Paul—two well known libertarian politicians.

As the middle class has declined in wealth, the oligarchy has inversely grown more organized with its ever tightening grip over the power structure. No path to control has been left untouched. Politicians don't even bother to write legislation anymore, even though they claim to. They don't even have to read what they vote on, as the machine filters everything for them. All they have to do is play their role like an actor on stage. Virtually all new laws of importance are written by the industries that want them passed. The puppet system moves their work directly to the front of the line. If the middle class is having any sort of serious problem, the politicians will go to their billionaire masters to ask them for ideas on what to do about it. There are virtually no true renegades in the system working on our behalf because if there were, they wouldn't be around for long. The power structure is carefully contained. The power struggles we witness on TV are not really struggles between the masses and government. The actual struggles that politicians are really sweating bullets over are between the billionaires themselves over the spoils of the middle class.

Recession

The incumbency rate in Congress is over 90%, meaning there is no true competition to get elected so long as you play by the rules. Congressmen can look forward to a very long career in power with very little fear of getting kicked out. Even though we have millions of smarter people who probably should be in politics, the competition is meant to be an unfair fight. In an effective oligarchy, the cream does not rise to the top. The United States has one of the highest incumbency reelection rates in the world.

The legislative goals of our government align perfectly with the goals of the billionaire, at all times. If the government veers off course, the elites will get offended, and the noise in the media will get really loud until the system gets back in line. It will be presented in such a way as to look like the will of the masses, but that is a false picture. Elites are well skilled in having their opinions presented under the guise of grass roots movements. The Orwellian media looks to their think tanks to project the talking points for public discourse. These *thought centers* work to control and limit thought processes to their particular ideology. Think tanks are basically ideology reinforcing machines.

Our corporate oligarchy is concerned about much more than just the United States. Their influence and sphere of control is virtually worldwide. Wherever they are making money or exploiting resources, they are maximizing their profit first and foremost. But it gives them the power to influence US policy toward the international priorities of multi-national corporations at the expense of more local concerns. They use our national power to achieve their international goals, while we mere locals are, in effect, on our own.

The elites are making money at accelerated rates thanks to several decades of being highly catered to by our fully *Reaganized* government. Because of the unbridling of our economic checks and balances, otherwise known as deregulation, elite profits have been able to increase at rates that far surpass what our middle class as a whole can ever hope to attain.

Part of the problem here is speed and the computer era has not helped. Politicians use computers for gerrymandering in order to make damned sure they can always get reelected. The voting pattern stats they track give incumbents a constant advantage. And if the ethnic mix changes or sentiment starts to move against them, they have the power to adjust the goal posts, and it's perfectly legal to do so. The oligarchy plays a similar game by studying banking procedures, political favors, and consumer patterns to make sure they are milking everybody and everything for all they can. They game the patent system, the legal system, and the tax system in ways that far exceed what the middle class can ever hope to pull off.

All this *fast* power leads to a system of speed and short term thinking that is perfect for accelerating large wealth to extreme wealth. A billionaire is not interested in waiting for 20 or 30 years to realize an investment idea. An international corporation wants a 20% gain every year. A corporate CEO is mostly worried about the next 5 years because that's most often when his tenure will end, and he wants to retire highly overpaid for his success. His elite stockholders and board members are all eager to make a fast profit. There is no force anywhere that dares to think of slowing down the speed of the system over a longer, more stable horizon.

40

Recession

As our economy runs up one huge bubble after another, one of the primary causes of this increase in volatility is the acceleration of economic speed to hyper-speed. Every economy, no matter how you run it, will be filled with mistakes, bad ideas and failures. But if you run an economy at an accelerated speed, those bad ideas will form much larger, temporary pockets of financial robbery prior to receiving their deserved failure. The desired pace of the oligarchy always has the gas pedal pushed down to the floorboard of the car. This is how the Russian oligarchy so successfully robbed their entire country of most of its major assets. The handoff was done lightening fast, giving their middle class no time at all to understand what was happening. By the time they figured it out, it was far too late. Speed is one of the favored tools for overpowering democracy, transparency, and fairness.

During the banking bubble from 2000 to 2007, our economic car was moving ahead at maximum speed. The Federal Reserve lowered interest rates at near 0% for no real logical reason. The buying of real estate was clipping along at an absurd pace, taking advantage of the cheap borrowing rates. Banks were lending out too much money. Home valuations began to inflate to the cheers of the home flippers. Clearly, when this bubble finally did pop in 2008, it became clear that all of these massive profits served absolutely no benefit whatsoever to the economy. The gains of this excess were a mirage. They existed *only* because somebody managed to rig up a really bad idea, and accelerate the movement of that idea to hyper-speed, to where the profit motive jumped way out in front of the failure filter. The middle class tends to get the collateral damage when the dust settles because ultimately it's always our piggy bank that is being robbed during the excess, and robbed once again to patch up the damage when the party ends. It's also our jobs being lost when the economy overgrows to unreasonable proportions. In a boom-bust market, the bust clears out far more qualified people than it should. The excessive demand creates excessive supply, and the vast majority of that excessive supply is usually middle class jobs.

Corporations are trying to move fast because they are trying to survive and compete. And if they move too slow somebody else might beat them. Their need for speed can be seen as entirely logical. It's easy to see how their priorities would infect our entire economic system. And that thinking has infiltrated how our government thinks. It's also affects how our economists set their own perceptions. They are all trying to move at the exact same pace as the power structure that owns them. It's a fine tuned corporate oligarchy rushing ahead to take over the world economy at a billionaire's preferred pace.

The primary contradiction between our oligarchy and our middle class is the issue of speed. The typical billionaire will complain that the middle class is not keeping up. We are not going back to college fast enough. We are not learning new skills fast enough. We are not looking for a new job after being laid off fast enough. We are not working 2 or 3 jobs fast enough. We are not saving enough. We are not spending enough. We are not borrowing enough. We are not keeping up with technology. They are sprinting along with their massive, wealthy army, and the middle class sits by, frozen and weary.

Recession

The classic billionaire has no way to visualize the world through middle class eyes. After all, he has multiple homes with six car garages. His children attend special schools with security guards. He has somebody making his breakfast every morning. His driver waits in the garage to drive him to work so he can read the paper on the way. His trophy wife is sleeping in late because her plastic surgery appointment is not until the afternoon. On the way to work he might stop by visit the young concubine he keeps at his secret condo. For some reason he is always able to arrive at work highly motivated. Everybody at work laughs a little too hard at his jokes. He thinks he is charismatic and funny. He thinks anybody in the world can accomplish the exact same life he has if they simply put their mind to it.

Your average middle class citizen has too many tools in his garage, if he is lucky enough to have a garage, so at least one of his cars has to be parked outside in the weather. There are things that need fixing that he is putting off until he has enough money saved up to deal with it. In many cases, he might be divorced, which means he's taking care of the kids by himself half the time while making child support payments. The ex-wife might be taking a pretty low paying job in order to monitor the kids until they get older. In a world where both parents work to support their family, divorce just makes it all even harder.

Millions of middle class workers have lost their job during at least one of the many recent market bubbles. The unemployment benefits are barely enough to pay the utility bill, but certainly not enough to pay for food, gas and mortgage. The only real saving grace is if he (or she) has a 401k from their previous job, then he can basically live off of his savings for one or two years in order to keep the home and keep his kids in school. Once his entire retirement savings is prematurely depleted, he might get a job nearly as good as the one he once had, but with less pay. He fears the next bubble might do him in again. He doesn't have a girlfriend because frankly he doesn't have enough free cash to date. If he is middle aged, then he's a little too old to start over with a whole new career. He has invested decades of his adult life in a particular specialty, driven down by excessive market bubbles. Had he known the bubbles were going to be the norm, he would have picked a different career. But at this point, any forced change to a different career would mean backing up to an income level of a 25 year old, working for a boss 15 years below his age. If he loses his job again he can always just give up, walk away from his mortgage, uproot his kids, and go live with his elderly parents. Or maybe he'll get a job in Saudi Arabia, where he can spend 5 years in a strange desert, separated from most of his family, trying to make up for lost time via slightly inflated pay. When the middle class spins its wheels in America, sometimes the only outlet to get ahead is in difficult, distant places outside the American economy.

This is the story of millions of Americans that is only beat by those who are far worse off and can't even afford to go to a dentist to get a cavity filled. There are untold numbers of Americans literally living the woods or in the streets. The hidden poverty in this country is there, and nobody is talking much about it. The elitist system is accustomed to ignoring the bottom rails. The problem is more of our middle class has been bumped down to join those lower rails than ever before.

Recession

The main variable that separates the middle class man from the billionaire is time. The billionaire has complete control over time to use as he pleases. He makes bets he can afford to lose. The middle class man is in a constant battle with time because as responsibilities begin to mount, there is never enough of it. When resources are limited, the management of time is the constant discipline that controls the realities of modest living. In hard times, he is forced to make bets that could virtually sink him if he loses.

Recessions are about time and the natural clock of life. Our economy is like a living, breathing thing that must expand and contract for the purposes of sorting out success and failure. And here is the little secret to recessions . . . *we need them*. We need the failure in order to find success. It's part of how progress and innovation operate. The problem with contemporary economic analysis is that it always focuses on success. But a more accurate view is there must be room for failure at all times. The real measure of risk is the space given for failure to exist as a common norm. Warren Buffet has said you should never make a bet you can't afford to lose. What he failed to add to that comment is the utter necessity of losing. There's a great deal of security when one can work within a system that allows for affordable losses.

If there's one thing our fast paced technological world has taught us, it is impossible to guess the future, and impossible to guess the winners and losers of the future. We have seen countless items go extinct very rapidly, like rotary phones, cassettes, 8 track tape and Kodak film. And as the changes come and go, as experiments succeed and fail, we have an economy that seeks to weed out the losers on the constant basis. The vast majority of our ideas fail, which is the undocumented part of life. We don't record how many times the baby falls down. We only record the day the baby manages to stand up. While the history books focus on the winners, it overlooks the mountain of failures that made those accomplishments possible.

Our American system is pretty good at weeding out bad ideas as we have one of the better bankruptcy systems in the world. It might be one of the few things that we do really well—the forgiveness of debt. At times, the government fails to recognize the need for it, and will constrain the system from failure in ways that are very harmful to the middle class. For example, student debt has swollen to huge numbers that may eventually collapse under its own weight. This bubble was partly created by the fact that this debt was given a very special status of not being able to fail while tuition rates have been steadily increasing well beyond the rate of income growth. Elites are able to run from their failed debts and they do so all the time. Donald Trump has certainly escaped his fair share of *ideas gone bad.* You don't hear him talk much about his history of bankruptcy. But in the case of middle class student debt, bankruptcy is not an option. That gives this debt a special status not seen since pre-modern times, where one can become a virtual slave to their bad debts forever, with no way out.

Our justice system is doing the same thing by putting people in jail who cannot afford to pay their fines, in effect, creating a debtor's prison. Or worse, there are jails that are charging service fees to those released. Prisons have become like private hotels. By inflicting a financial trap on those members of society who can least afford to get trapped, we are denying the critical fact that all economic models must have a failure outlet so people can restart from their mistakes. The lower you sit on the social scale, the harder it is to get any traction or security from falling down. If the middle class is having trouble finding work, imagine how hard it must be for ex-convicts or the homeless. The overall system has been getting less and less tolerant of failure at the bottom, and more and more accommodating of failure at the top.

Nearly every market bubble crisis this economy has ever known has been the result of mislabeling risks for a period of time. The S&L crisis of the early 1980s was a major banking crisis caused specifically by an attempt to misallocate risk. The 2008 banking crisis was caused by a derivatives scheme that misrepresented the real risk. Large bubbles in the economy, as seen in the 1970s oil bubble, 1980s junk bond bubble, or the 2001 tech bubble are damaging to the middle class because they convert the recession mechanism into a depression mechanism. This is like taking a human heart and making it pump twice as much blood. It's unnatural, dangerous, and can cause a middle class heart attack.

Elites have grumbled quite a bit about our government extending unemployment benefits during the 2008 crisis because they believe the middle class needs more pain to induce them to find a job. They hold an amoral belief system that naturally fears any economic actions that appear to be based on pity. They believe in tough love for the masses. But when elites get in trouble, they tend to expect a very tender heart.

47

Huge drops in the market are caused because we allowed for huge increases in the market. Rapid gains are celebrated until they fail, which they always do, and then the pain begins for all those who can't afford to feel it. The elitist theory believes that a market cannot move ahead without some incentive to help get it moving along; thus, they pester politicians to help spike the system. This doesn't make a lot of sense in the middle class world because we don't really need any help being creative or innovative. We don't need any help getting motivated. The only thing we really need is protection from elitists with big ideas that will ultimately create dangerous whipsaw cycles.

For the past three centuries, the United States has been enduring recessions at a very constant rate. No amount of modernization has ever stopped it, nor should it. Unfortunately, our current elitist Federal Reserve thinks it is doing everybody a favor by preventing or eliminating recessions. The more years that pass by without a recession, the more pride they have of their accomplishment. But that's a really bad idea because without any recession, we are only creating an even bigger bubble that will only sting a lot worse when it finally pops. It's not possible to have a recession free world, it's not healthy, and it's not desirable. Instead, the Federal Reserve should be measuring its success by how steady and even it can keep the heartbeat of the economy beating. A long series of regular interval, mild recessions would be the optimum pulse for any market. These are periods where everybody can quickly verify their decisions, and adjust to any errors in judgment. Most ideas fail, and we need to see these failures quickly, while they are small and relatively painless.

The middle class sometimes needs to adjust career patterns, which can only be done in a stable environment. Unlike elites, we don't have the resources to make these adjustments during a depression.

The billionaire perspective admires how well a system can create new millionaires. That's the common idol worship and self importance that is to be expected from an elitist point of view. The elitist thinks in heroic terms because psychologically he sees himself as a hero. What is missing from billionaire indoctrination is the fact that the most important hero of the entire clan actually has a name, and he is almost always missing from the conversation. His name is *the middle class*. Why should that not be the ultimate hero of our economic philosophy? Bringing the poor into the middle class is far more important, and far more productive, than counting the number of heads that move into the elite. For a study of countries that have successfully escalated their millionaire population, Mexico and Russia would be ideal examples.

Because the American middle class has become the biggest pot of gold in the history of civilization, it has turned into the world's most prominent asset for the elites to exploit. Because we are so large in number, we have a body that can bleed out for decades before anybody will finally see that only a corpse remains. All third world countries are run by governments that are masters of exploitation. They can only exploit their poor because they have no real middle class, but suffice it to say, there is no population too poor to be abused by their masters. There doesn't come a day when the corrupt crony says, "Jeez, maybe we should stop already!"

External conditions can and do happen, which can cause any recession to be worse than normal. But if we are under the constant discipline of small recessions, that will help prepare the population to always be modest with their money, build up some savings, and be ready to handle risk. Unfortunately, modesty does not sit well with those calling the shots today.

When the Federal Reserve boosted home building with artificially low interest rates, this fueled a lack of discipline into the market, increasing greed and overconfidence. Risk models started to tilt into unreal scenarios that got overextended to the point that people started to believe the fantasy. This false exuberance set up the country for a large down cycle that middle class people were simply not prepared to endure. When the crash of 2008 occurred, millions of people lost their jobs, their savings, and their homes. Thousands of bankers were laid off. Thousands of architects were laid off. Thousands of construction companies had to shut down their operations. Thousands of manufacturers saw their revenue streams drop by 50%. The chain reaction was both enormous and needless. Even school districts started losing money, and many teachers were needlessly let go, forcing class sizes to increase beyond their healthy maximum. The smart money saw this problem coming and completely got out of the real estate market prior to the bust. But middle class workers don't have the luxury of *getting out of the way* of an economic tidal wave. They are tied down with a mortgage, kids, debts, and life.

The Federal Reserve and wealthy politicians are all blind to the reality of what works for the best long term interest of the middle class. They are so busy trying to find ways to temporarily boost the economy that they scarcely have any understanding for the need to tamp it down. A stable economy will allow for creativity and intellectualism to find a healthy amount of space to exist. The concern about health, rent, or where your next meal is coming from is typically the concern of the very poor. That is a life that has no time to think about literature, science, saving the planet, or coming up with great ideas to help others. A stable middle class has time to think, relax, help others, and react to important problems. And the vast majority of these activities are done in people's homes, in their spare time, devoid of any participation from corporations, billionaires, think tanks, or trade agreements. One of the most important research labs America has ever had sits in the garages, living rooms, and home offices of the average American family.

The middle class has to work on a very slow clock that is entirely generation based. It takes a full generation to raise a family. We typically only go to college once. We have to pick a career, which is a life setting business decision. And we have to try to make that decision work for the next 40 years. Unlike a spoiled billionaire, a middle class citizen has to make a single big bet with his entire life. He has to make a long term investment that must survive all of the craziness and nonsense of the market. Until the government and its policy makers start getting sensitive to the middle class clock, we won't have much luck in getting the economy tuned to the proper pulse that is healthiest for our survival. The free-for-all boom-bust clock only serves the rich. The boring clock that rarely changes is the ultimate middle class time piece.

The middle class is basically a very long term 40 year bond. The elites treat the middle class like a cheap, short term penny stock bought on a day trade. The Fed obsesses over the stock market, artificially increasing risks with lower rates, while the bond market is being shifted to a perilous position that has never been seen before. In many ways, our somewhat fantasy bond market says a lot about the falsified reality of our middle class. Both are being manipulated to artificially low rates near 0% in an effort to boost a short term bubble economy. It's a formula for failure escalation because real risk has become impossible to measure.

MC2: Steady, modest recessions are a vital ingredient to middle class economic stability.

The Cost: Artificial market stimulation over the past 40 years has created millions of unnecessary shifts in middle class career planning. Educated individuals are forced to shift to less challenging work, lower pay or career reversal. The underutilization of the middle class is likely to be 25% below its appropriate value due to elitists artificially inducing instability into the career market. This factor can only be measured over entire generations; therefore, it would take nearly a century to get an accurate estimate of the actual potential.

THREE

Strong Money

There's another word for 0%. It's called stealing.

In the early 1990s, JP Morgan was starting to get fancy with the derivatives concept, finding new forms of financial instruments they could market to their clients. This drew very little notice from the media at that time. But there was one lone exception who was not at all impressed. Jim Rogers, a well known independent investor began to warn of the dangers of derivatives. On CNBC, he explicitly said, "Remember the word derivative because some day we are all going to hear it in the news." As he put it, "A derivative is nothing more than another method for increasing debt." As it turned out, Rogers called this perfectly. Perhaps even he did not realize it might take another 15 years for derivatives to evolve into a serious problem involving several leading multinational institutions in one of the worst Wall Street catastrophes of all time. All the same, his long forgotten, barely noticed concerns proved valid.

The word *derivative* infamously showed up in the news when the banking system seized up in 2008. Treasury Secretary Tim Geithner worked very hard to bail out the guilty banks and insurance companies with massive amounts of middle class tax dollars. He was convinced that not saving them would cause a world-wide depression and massive economic catastrophe. Somehow, he was unable to see that our banking industry had grown to a size far bigger than what our economy actually needed. Reducing the amount of banking in this country to normal historic proportions would have been a good thing. The economic cemetery is chocked full deceased banks of all sizes. The earth still spins. There are ways to dismantle even large banks without directly harming small depositors. The government does it all the time. But Geithner obviously lacked both the courage and the ideology to stand up to elite power and say no. He determined that these banks were simply *too big to fail*.

This transfer of middle class money to save irresponsible bankers should be remembered in the history books as one of the greatest financial robberies in all of world history. There's a saying that corrupt governments will privatize profits to their elite buddies, but if their buddies fail, they will socialize the losses back to the tax payer. Poor countries do this all the time. The United States revealed its own immorality by choosing to protect its incompetent insiders.

Geithner has since tried to sell his apologetic policies in his new book *Stress Test*, stating that we have to swallow our pride and do distasteful things for the good of the system. His extraordinary narrowness of vision is emblematic of the kind of restricted ideology that creates these kinds of problems in the first place. He is the perfect amoral tool, stripped of all moral judgment—a perfectly designed robot to the system.

Strong Money

When McChesney left the chair of the Federal Reserve in 1970, the golden age of the Fed and its protection of the middle class came to an end. A new era emerged where politicians could sway our financial guardians to short term, selfish interests. Nixon was eager to gain this additional authority through his new Fed chairman and political whipping boy Arthur Burns. Dovish, loose monetary policy and inflation quickly took root. Things quickly went downhill for the next eight years. President Carter appointed William Miller to fill the position in 1978, and he only lasted one year. Things went from bad to worse as the American dollar began to collapse in value around the world. At this point, inflation was getting totally out of hand. This was the opening stages of the long term middle class slide from 1968.

In desperation, President Carter decided to swing the opposite direction and appoint a hawkish Fed chairman with some courage. His advisors begged him not to do it because they knew any sort of hawkish monetary policy would create short term pain and cost him the election. It was political suicide. But Carter was more concerned about the economy than his job, so he went ahead with the appointment of Paul Volcker, who stated he would raise interest rates as high as necessary to end inflation. This appointment was a truly rare act of patriotic courage. Volcker did exactly what he said he would do. The medicine was applied, causing short term pain. It did cost Carter the election. And by the time the economy began to recover from Volcker's disciplined approach, Reagan was there to take all the credit for something he had absolutely nothing to do with.

The Reagan administration ultimately fired Volcker in 1987 because they did not feel he was sufficiently on board with their strong desire to deregulate absolutely everything. Reagan thought government was the cause of all problems. So they brought in the ultimate elitist dove Alan Greenspan to once again help give away the farm to the private elite sector. Sadly, Greenspan had been given a fantastic springboard to operate from because Volcker's good work had set up the country for a very solid future. There was essentially more to steal. This allowed Greenspan to operate with many additional years of robbery before any real pain would be detected by the masses. Meanwhile, his overstimulation of Wall Street was met with adulation by the financial press. Thus began a completely renewed era of dovish monetary policy, artificially low interest rates, and massive government debt. To this day, it still has not stopped as Greenspan, Bernanke, and Yellen are all carved from the same exact mold. There is no discernible difference in their policies. All are trained to operate in lockstep with Geithner-like protectionism for the elite establishment.

The real irony here is that McChesney was a humble man who felt his intellect was limited. He feared the markets that he managed, and yet his management record was rather phenomenal. His hawkish monetary policy helped to support the greatest middle class and the greatest distribution of wealth the world has ever known. In contrast, Greenspan and Bernanke were far less humble, far more overconfident with their intellect, and far more willing to tamper with monetary policy, basically contradicting everything

McChesney ever stood for. Yet, looking at their legacy, they have presided over an economy where the middle class is in a far weaker state, savings rates have deteriorated, debt has skyrocketed, and the rich have never been richer. How many times do we have to see the inverse relationship between money and humility to get the message?

The government likes to play this little game with our currency called money printing. Since they control the printing presses they can basically print up money out of thin air by increasing the supply of money in the marketplace. There are several different ways they can do this. Recent Fed policy has been focused on buying up their own bonds in an effort to manipulate the bond market, artificially lowering bond rates to stimulate additional risk taking in the market. Just think about it for a minute. Your own government issues bonds, and then your own government buys its bonds back to falsify the market demand. If the word Enron is starting to creep into your consciousness about now, then that's probably a good sign that you have a financial conscience. But Bernanke and Yellen use academic garb to support this absurd approach to stimulating the economy. It hasn't worked.

The biggest losers of artificially low interest rates are the elderly because they have the biggest need for interest income from their modest savings. Cheap money rewards debtors over savers, which is why our country is getting buried in debt. It draws money out of both the people and their government, maximizing all debt, and shifting all asset ownership to elite, corporate power. In the 1950s, McChesney explained in great detail how dovish currency policy would be harmful to the small saver and the middle class. Absolutely everything he warned could go wrong did go wrong under Greenspan and Bernanke.

All governments like to inflate their currency. By and large, the more corrupt countries will inflate far more than the more honest ones. The honesty of a government can often be judged by its inflation level. Responsible governments will keep their currency as stable as possible. Irresponsible governments constantly steal value from their money because they can't resist the elitist demands on the public piggy bank.

Artificially low interest rates are a way of secretly taxing the rest of us. Politicians love it because they don't have to ask for as much in additional taxes. They will simply extract value from your currency instead. They also can avoid making any difficult choices because with an effective money printing scheme, they can reward all their buddies by running up more debt. With near zero percent interest rates, the government debt is not really costing the government much of anything. Cheap money has become an alternative to functional government. It's a win for politicians and the rich, and a loss for the middle class who ultimately get stuck with the tab in the form of debt traps from which they cannot escape. And to add more insult to the process, the government routinely moves the goal posts in the market data to underreport true inflation levels.

The comment made regularly in business circles since the 2008 crash is that corporations are sitting on piles of money and not spending it. Elites are sitting on piles of cash, as never before. But the one group in this story that is strapped for cash is the middle class. Our economy is supposed to be a three part puzzle of workers, bosses, and corporations, but only two parts of this puzzle seem to have more cash than they know what to do with. There appears to be plenty of liquidity in certain circles, but try as our government might to stimulate the economy, all of the stimulation money keeps ending up in elite pockets.

A cheaper dollar has resulted in other countries copying our lead in order to keep up. Since we are trying to flood the world market in excessive dollars, other governments have done the same thing in order to prevent their exports from being underpriced. This exponentially increases world-wide money printing as other governments repeat our mistake. As world debt escalates, this can easily lead to something really bad later on.

One of the other results we see from several decades of excessive liquidity is an excessive amount of banking in the financial system. If we compare today to the 1960s, banking has more than doubled as a percentage of the economy. Historically, banking has ranged between 2% to 4% of the overall economy. It got up to 6% right before the Great Depression, before crashing back down to 2%. Today, banking is in excess of 8% of the economy and still growing. More banking exists because the government has helped to inflate liquidity. We are in a record setting liquidity bubble that will someday pop with massive consequences. The tragic bust of 2008 might very well have been a mild dress rehearsal for what will eventually result from our ongoing monetary excess.

By expanding our financial industry into something far bigger than needed, banking has become an aggressive business that holds much of the middle class hostage to credit card debt, with plenty of incentives to keep the game going on forever. Most of the middle class has monthly credit card payments that exceed many of their other monthly utility bills. Like a drug dealer getting more addicts addicted, this market has become something the banks don't want to let go of, and the government has done nothing to break the cycle. It bleeds billions of unproductive dollars out of the middle class year after year. This condition did not exist in 1968, when consumer credit was very hard to come by.

This would be an appropriate time to place a tombstone to celebrate the life of an old friend of the middle class. His name was the Glass-Steagall Act, born 1933, died 1999, may he rest in peace. This legislation was passed in response to the Great Depression to keep banks under control from excessive speculation. After it was repealed in 1999, the real party got started up again, and the ensuing speculation far exceeded anything ever seen in the Roaring 20s. The leverage of debt has gone far beyond the value of our entire country's economy, multiple times over. Money printing and debt has been taken to a whole new level never before tested by any historical reference point. Our national GDP is around $50 trillion, yet our banking debt instruments may be in the hundreds of trillions of dollars. Nobody knows for sure because so much of the more creative instruments in place are not well documented or publicized.

The Fed has not been very transparent with the condition of the major banks they are currently protecting from failure. They had to be sued in court to force the release of their bail-out money. They appealed the ruling multiple times to avoid disclosure. They feared bank runs, so they did not want the public to know which banks were weak and which ones were strong. It's rather ironic that our free market system does not want us to see the accounting of bank failure. It's even more ironic that these are publically traded corporations, with stock holders who invest their money into something that apparently does not have to honestly disclose its own bailout status. The deeper this absurd financial hole gets, the more games the government has to play to protect their masters from harm.

In a simple banana republic, where government theft and cronyism is rampant, financial volatility is common and wreaks havoc on the average citizen. The United States is able to get away with far more manipulation because our currency is a world base currency, which affords a lot more slack in the rope before a major collapse. And just like any irresponsible kid, our Federal Reserve is able to push debt limits far beyond what any average analyst would have ever thought possible. They play with fire today, yet the longer they get away with it, the more tempted they are to believe that they are geniuses for getting away with it. They keep finding more complex math to justify how perfectly safe and sound their practice is. Over time, they cease to be properly paranoid about the danger and continue to push the limits even further. This numbing effect toward risk always increases during major market bubbles, where the insane starts to look sane up until the moment it all collapses. The day will come when people will look back on our contemporary Federal Reserve as completely insane.

The American banking industry has never been very stable. For over 200 years banks have been going broke on a constant basis. You would think that banks would be more stable than the rest of the economy. But if anything, they might be even less stable than their own customers. Just because bankers are specialists in the field of money does not mean they are better equipped to survive in the marketplace. In reality, they stand as leveraged money to the economy they lend to, so they are actually weaker than the markets they serve. Their long, constant failure rate would certainly point to that reality, and thus there is the obvious need to keep banks held to a much higher standard than the average business.

Markets have always been crazy, rough and tumble places. In the 1800s, bank failures were more common than today because there was no real system in place to protect depositors, and no Glass-Steagall Act. There was no Federal Reserve. Bank runs were common during market panics and even the backing of money with gold was often disrupted. The one thing that remained amazingly stable during the entire 19th century was the American currency itself. Despite a massive Civil War, and a number of other challenges, the US dollar was amazingly stable in value. The gold standard helped to keep it that way. It's pretty easy to see the stability if you track the value of gold in dollars throughout that century. The value of gold barely ever changed for more than a century. The beauty of this stability was that a simple farmer could hold some cash in his home for years without losing any real purchasing power. With a currency that strong, even holding it without interest was ok in a fairly deflationary century.

In general, the 1800s provided protection and stability for the mostly rural population of that time. This was an amazing accomplishment, all done because the US government was never real fond of high debts or currency manipulation. Perhaps the constant failure of banks kept them alert to the fact that currency was important and worth protecting, even if banks could not hack survival. Alexander Hamilton set the example at the very beginning, defending the need for honest, government credit, and President Grant reset that trend as a prominent Republican mantra after the Civil War. The decision to keep America frugal was a primary saving grace to the country for an entire century.

From 1793 to 1833, an ounce of gold stayed at $19.39. Then for nearly 100 years, from 1834 to 1932, it stayed at $20.67, with only a few bumps and changes along the way. It got up to $47 in 1864, but given the historical context of that time, one should expect a few short surprises like that. But overall, that's pretty amazing stability for a currency to remain relatively unchanged for such an extraordinary period of time. Since the invention of the Federal Reserve in 1913, we have been living in an inflationary world every since. The price of gold, currently exceeding $1300 an ounce at the printing of this book, rises forever. These days, gold holds far better value than our dollar.

The one thing our middle class needs from a currency is stability. Because of the unpredictability of the future, finding something solid to grab onto as a store of value is exponentially more important. It's like finding a buoy in the middle of an ocean. We can't stop the waves, but we can plant something down that doesn't move, to help give us a point of reference.

About the only thing our government can really nail down (if it wanted to) would be our currency. It is possible to maintain a strong stable currency, but the government has to be willing to do it, understanding the wisdom of doing so. Currency must serve as a solid amoral post that rarely moves, so that everything dependent on it can find its rightful position within the free market system. In a modern world of rapid change, the anchoring stability of currency is even more important now than it was in a more static economy.

The American government, since the time of McChesney left his job at the Fed, has had no desire to keep our currency stable, strong, or safe. They have played with it and toyed with it on a pretty constant basis. And all of the change and fluctuation has done constant damage to the middle class. It has never occurred to anybody at the Fed what the most important relationship is between the middle class and money. The lack of change and strength in value are the two most critical attributes of responsible monetary policy—the two very things our contemporary Fed has been the least respectful of.

What's good for the middle class is also good for business in general because a stable, strong currency helps keep the market calm and stable. It makes the future more predictable, and risk calculations get easier. Businesses can plan the future with greater ease. Instability hurts business because people are not sure what they are getting into, then everything becomes a crap shoot. The risk of hiring increases. The valuation of assets becomes suspect when everything is under constant manipulation. And best of all, strong money stimulates the will to save.

In banana republic countries, cash and currency can be hard to find. Their grocery stores tend to minimize how much cash they keep on hand. Nobody wants to hold cash in poor countries because time is their enemy. Rich people in poor countries will invest in real estate, or other tangible objects to store wealth because they don't trust the banks to protect their savings. They end up having to dodge currency with other artificial substitutes for storing value, including the use of international banks outside the country.

Talk of higher rates and stronger currency is blasphemy to our power structure of today. They have way too much intellectual investment to let this go. When systems get this broken, the only real fix is usually catastrophic failure. That's often what it takes to break a bad ideology. Direction does not get reversed willingly. Instead, they will step on the accelerator and speed up the current system, imagining that they simply have not done enough of what they are already doing. They will fight debt with more debt. The will fight lower interest rates with negative interest rates. They will fight failed banks with bailouts. Being wrong is hard on cronies.

The currency infection has also hit our stock exchange, where the exchange itself has become a kind of side business to leaches of the system. When Michael Lewis exposed the game of high speed trading in "Flash Boys," he introduced us to the one lone hero from Canada who sought to make the game honest—the founder of IEX Brad Katsuyama. Katsuyama discovered how insiders were gaming the system for secret advantage. It took a fair amount of high tech investigating to discover the scam. Sadly, the scam he found is perfectly legal. Companies assigned to help the public buy stock were secretly manipulating prices within fractions of a second in order to skim money from the exchange. Katsuyama sought to out-market the dishonesty by trying to craft an alternative trading model that could stop the high speed cheating, putting all traders back on a level playing field. However, blind amorality has become so pervasive in our elitist economic system that Katsuyama's morality has been viewed with incredible suspicion by many market insiders.

But this leads us to an even bigger problem that nobody is discussing. Day traders are not investors. An investor is somebody who buys stock in the company because they believe it is undervalued, they believe it has a bright future, and they want to go along for the ride for a period of time hoping to make a better return on their money. And short seller is also a participant who believes the company will go down in value. These two opposites help to keep the buyer and sellers honest in the trading of stock. In either case, they are betting on a business trend over a period of weeks, months, or years. But the day trader is not interested in making an investment based on the activity of a company. They are looking to sell something almost as fast as they buy it. And it has reached a point where owning a company of only a few seconds is time enough. They are looking for the defects in the system to simply profit from the defect. It's similar to the ticket scalper who rushes to the front of the line to buy tickets to a show, not because he wants to see the show, but because he wants to turn around and resell that ticket to you for an inflated price.

Day trading is disrespectful to the system because our trading system is also a currency. A trader brings no value to the hard work of others trying to be successful. All the trader can really do is rob the system of some of its value and increase the volatility of the market. Benign purchasing is not benign. It's misleading to the normal calculations used to place value on actual buying and selling between real investors.

It would be super easy to stop this nonsense by heavily taxing short term investments. It would also be possible to slow the system down if we wanted to. For example, if the government required it, we could say that all stock purchases must be held a minimum of 24 hours. We could debate what the most appropriate time limit should be. It could be 1 minute, 1 hour, 1 day, or 1 month. Ultimately, any of these limits would probably be healthy to consider because it would put the day traders out of business. It would force everybody who wants to buy stock to become an actual investor. It would slow down and stabilize the trading system that needs to serve serious investors. If you think about it, this is how mutual funds already operate. You can only buy them at closing price each day, and many of them will penalize customers who want to trade out too quickly. They cannot implement proper investment strategies without a stable pool of money to invest with.

Super short investment practices create a gamesmanship mentality that is not good for business, and not good for the middle class. It's disrespectful, and the market purists are apparently blind to the immorality of the practice. If the government were serious about wanting to increase investment in the system, they would first need to learn how to distinguish exactly what a real investor looks like.

If you study the real origins of World War I and II, they began with decades of wild economic speculation that took place over most of Europe in the late 1800s. When the over-speculation began to fail around the turn of the century, the failure of government power eventually led to war. The hyper-financialization we are witnessing today can lead to some very dangerous consequences down the road because incompetent power, once exposed, can be very dangerous when it gets desperate for scapegoats.

Changes in interest rates should always be very small, and kept at a snail's pace. Interest rates should never be artificially low. The Federal Reserve should be so slow and boring that the media ceases to pay attention to what they do. The Federal Reserve of today has been trying to basically become a day trader. Their involvement in the marketplace has become so excessive the markets are living on their every move. As long as we continue down this volatile path of short trades, zero percent currency, interest rate manipulation, high debt ratios, and massive Fed intervention, the middle class will always be at extreme risk.

Finances are most stable when they are kept very simple and clear. There is no need to get fancy with money. Banks are not a place for heavy growth or excessive innovation. Banking should not even be conceived of as an industry. It is not the proper place for million dollar bonus checks. Banking is ultimately an extension of our currency. And both need to be kept boring and simple. Any problems we suffer with banking are going to be closely tied with problems we have with our currency. The two run hand in hand.

When banks combine their complex debt instruments with the government's goal of cheap money, we have ripe conditions for a grass fire. Somewhere along the way our government forgot what currency is. It's supposed to be an unbiased third party—an amoral storage of value. It is *not* supposed to be a market *participant*.

If we could unwind the clock and go back to 1987, when Reagan was ready to appoint a new Federal Reserve chairman, let's imagine what might have happened had we avoided this whole elitist mistake called Alan Greenspan and Ben Bernanke. What would the middle class world look like now had somebody with McChesney's morality and common sense been installed? A lot of factors could have turned out a whole lot better. Had the rates on money stayed pretty constant and fairly valued, we would be looking at an entirely different world today. For one thing, the government could not have run up their debts into the trillions of dollars because the interest payments on this debt would have quickly been too prohibitive. Had rates remained strong, the middle class would have far more savings in the bank, and far less credit card debt. The elderly would be more fairly rewarded for their savings. Bubbles and volatility in the market would have been far less because when money is more expensive, cheap gambles become more expensive. Strong money has to be smart money. The failure filter, which is critical to our innovative capacity, would be far more effective under a strong currency. The 2008 crash would have been avoided because the real estate bubble would have never happened. A strong currency for the past 40 years would have forced discipline on an undisciplined world.

People around the world would want their money invested here as a safe haven. Wars would be harder to finance, thus, we would have less military aggression. Countries would be forced to compete with our strong money policies. Banking would have stayed at only 2% to 4% of our economy because excessive liquidity would be financially impossible. The financial security of our kids and grandkids would be far more certain. Not a bad trade off.

Unfortunately, that bright scenario is only a fairy tale. Our parents were lucky enough to live under a responsible Fed. We got stuck with the elitist rotten apples.

MC3: A strong middle class must have a strong, stable currency backed by a boring, uncreative banking system.

The Cost: The entire distribution of jobs in our country would be different under a responsibly run currency. There would be far less banking and far more manufacturing and export. Middle Class wealth could easily be 50% higher living under a stubbornly strong, uneventful currency. This is truly the ultimate, self-disciplining, amoral tool when properly protected because it prevents a huge collection of other problems from ever gaining momentum.

FOUR

Competition

The lack of competition among the elite is exactly where nobody is looking.

The average payout to the typical American CEO is 200 to 500 times higher than the average worker. In other words, if the corporation's average worker makes $70,000, the CEO might make over $14 million per year. Our so called free market capitalist model says that $14+ million per year is a competitive salary for a CEO. In a country with millions of educated workers, with some of the best universities on the planet, there are apparently no other qualified people willing to take on this role for less. If we are to believe in the principles of free market capitalism, this means that if they had offered a paltry $5 million per year, they would not be able to attract sufficient "talent" to take this job. If you think something smells a little funny, it should.

Looking back at the golden decade of the 1960s, our CEO's were making on average about 35 to 50 times more money than their average worker. If the average worker made $70k (today's dollars), then the CEO made $2.5 to $3.5 million per year. Do you think it's possible to find a really bright person to run a company for a mere $3.5 million? These more reasonable ratios were the norm in the United States back in 1968. These more reasonable ratios are *still* the norm in the rest of the world today.

When questions about excessive pay are brought up in the media, everybody just scratches their head in confusion, unable to find a reasonable explanation for all the overvaluation. It doesn't take a math expert to see that a boss of a company could possibly be worth 30 to 50 times more money than his average employee. That actually sounds within reason. But who besides a demigod is worth 300 to 500 times more money than the productive capacity of his own staff? In the warped American system we live in today, unreasonable amounts of money are being squandered at the top. Elites like to point to wasteful spending in the economy. Well, paying way too much to way too few rich people is also squandering and wasteful. It serves the rest of us no use at all to be investing in a billionaire's great grandkids while he is busy finding clever new ways to use up the future earnings of our grandkids.

What is so freaking special about American corporate leaders? And why is it that when they do incompetent work, they get paid tens of millions of dollars to be fired? Where did this culture of the golden parachute come from? Why does the American system so badly want to overpay those who least need the help? The answer to this problem has everything to do with the sinking conditions of the American middle class.

We are supposed to compete in the marketplace where we get measured for our value. Our contribution to society is worth a certain amount of money relative to our peers. When you interview for that new job, the employer looks at 20 other resumes and picks you. Your salary is determined by what the other 19 candidates would have taken to feed *their* kids. You will accept the offer because you don't have any second offers. That's called competition. Of course, these days the job probably isn't as challenging because you are not really able to find a job that truly matches your previous years of experience and knowledge. You had already invested years or decades building up extensive knowledge in a field that was destabilized and destroyed by the huge market bubble the Fed created, leaving a large crater in your life where the explosion went off. But like a good middle class soldier, you take your medicine and work a lower paying, less challenging job because our "efficient" marketplace put you there. If this sounds familiar to you, you are probably one of the lucky ones. Millions of people in this country are working below their effective capacity at little choice of their own.

The middle class can adjust to pretty much any kind of market you throw at them, so long as you stop trying to change it. If you can let the economy stand still long enough for the rest of us to focus in on it with our bifocals, we can all figure out how to live in it. Unfortunately, those with real macro-power over our economy keep trying to boost it along by moving around trillions of dollars to key, "strategic places," putting the middle class on shaky ground. It shifts all of us over to cheap wooden boats floating around in the ocean. No matter what we choose for smart security, it has become a crap shoot put on by uninvited game makers looking for special, short-term advantages.

The fact that the rich have gained more ground than everybody else tells us something about how this current system is actually working. The competitive structure at the elite level is broken because it has become hugely overvalued for a very long period of time. The middle class has become severely undervalued. The rich do not have to compete hard enough at their level, while the middle class is suffering from over-competition at ours. Our market is misplacing priorities from very damaging imbalances.

An elitist society sincerely believes that dollars equate with wisdom. In private, they honestly think they are smarter than the rest of us and more competent at running the country. That is why they tend to possess no guilt about exercising their additional influence over the country's power structure. If you refer back to the comical memo written by Justice Powell, or better yet, listen to the secret recording of Mitt Romney talking to his fellow arrogant elites over a fundraising dinner, it's quite obvious they don't think too highly of the *little people* living beneath them. It's a bit of a slave owner's mentality.

In the years between 1932 and 1968, the taxes on the rich escalated to the highest progressive rates ever implemented in this country's history. In the Eisenhower years, it was upwards of 90% in the late 1950s. This is one of the reasons our middle class became so strong because those who were far more comfortable were expected to contribute far more to the government. By tamping down the elites with significant transfer payments, that helped to adjust value back to the middle class, giving them a stronger competitive position in the overall mix of the economy.

Competition

Since the 1960s, taxing the rich slowly began to fall out of fashion. Lowering taxes became the new dogma, which was supposed to create a richer world by letting the rich hold on to more of their money. And that story proved to be true. It did create a richer world . . . for the *rich*. The data today clearly shows that it did not create anything for the rest of us. The establishment will dispute this argument like a broken record despite all the evidence to the contrary. Conventional belief among conservatives has been that taxing the rich does not make any difference because it is believed that within a generation of two, all of that accumulated wealth will disintegrate anyway. And there is some truth to this in many cases. A lot of wealth does get divided and squandered by inheritance over time. But it is not so true near the very top of the ladder, where various oligarchs are building up enough wealth to form their own private empires.

The only argument ever mentioned about income tax rates is the negative effect it has on the business community. But the entire discussion about taxes tends to miss the point on what it does to our social structure. A progressive tax system has a very important effect on the issue of competition *within* the elite class that is completely absent from current economic theory. A progressively higher tax on the rich makes it harder to *be* rich and harder to *stay* rich. And that is a critical issue which is actually more important than where those taxes get transferred to. Being rich doesn't have to be impossible. But being rich should not be made easier by the government. There is no good reason to shroud it and protect it. Most rich people believe in tough love, so let them be first in line to prove it. By increasing the difficulty on both their income and their capital gains, we are in a sense making the position of the wealthy far more competitive *among* the wealthy. This makes *excess* currency more expensive than *necessity* currency, as it should be.

Our current system has destroyed the competitive aspect of being wealthy because those at the top don't have to work very hard to make incredible amounts of money with their money. The system is basically over-rewarding them for their effort. Giving the rich a free ride eventually creates a damaging moral effect on the overall free market system. We see that result today.

As one moves up the social ladder in an effective democracy, the challenges for procuring more wealth *should* be increasingly difficult. The competition for those extra dollars should get increasing difficult. After all, we need our best and brightest at the top of the ladder, and the one way to assure that is to keep making the prize incrementally more difficult to attain.

It's really a wonder there is any money left over for the middle class because the amount of waste in so many of our sectors is incredibly overgrown and overvalued. The concept of free market capitalism should be viewed with tremendous skepticism because it is assumed to be efficient. But there is obviously a lot of interference going on with the supply mechanism due to elite corruption. Oligarchs and corporate power are finding ways to overvalue product in countless different sectors, forming multiple bubbles in our economy that can never pop because they are too well protected, and many times too well hidden from view. The free market is captured by the elite. A more appropriate term would be free market elitism.

Competition

Fixing heavily engrained problems will require changing our thought process about economics in fundamental ways. We have very inefficient systems that are funneling more and more money to fewer and fewer sources. The beneficiaries of this power are naturally going to think the system is perfectly efficient. They have plenty of reason to love the economic model as it is. At the very top of power, you will always find extremely aggressive resistance to change or even to being challenged in any way.

Those who have power have resources to invest a great deal of money into social indoctrination to induce all others to cooperate with the status quo. The higher up you go in the economic food chain, the stronger the indoctrination gets. Hannah Arendt used to say that the most indoctrinated person in the world is the President of the United States. The very center of power is where thought is most heavily controlled. Naturally, the most open minded to change tend to be the very poor, who have plenty of reason to not love the current system. As our country continues to accumulate more poor people, the skepticism from below will continue to rise.

Elite intellectuals will argue that we cannot, or should not, pick and choose winners in the marketplace. The problem is our government has been picking the same elites as the same winners, over and over again. It would be nice to see the government pick the middle class every now and then as a priority, but it very rarely does. In fact, virtually never does it ever really pick the middle class as its very first priority. Corporate interests have high jacked almost all government thought, assuming to speak on behalf of the rest of us. That hasn't worked out so well.

If the middle class is being undervalued, it will be necessary to restore some value, even if we have to do it artificially with transfer payments. It will hurt some sectors, but restoring proper value to the middle class is the best single investment the government could ever make, even though we theoretically have the weakest lobbying department to get our point across. The nice thing about progressive taxes is they do not target specific industries, but rather excessive profits. Think of it as an insurance payment against a future bubble pop. If super high incomes are coming to a particular sector, which is always hard to predict when and where it will happen, but if the gains are truly high, the tax will also be high, which will have a natural stabilizing effect on the bubble formations. The Fed tries to do this with monetary policy instead, which unfairly tortures the poor and middle class while piling on even more reward to the least deserving.

The 1960s economy was born out of an era of massive transfer payments and strong banking regulation. It was brought down later by Reagan style skepticism against government itself, lowering taxes, raising debts, and relaxing banking regulations. The benefits handed over to elites proved to be very damaging to the middle class who had so greatly depended on government to help keep all the players honest, out of debt, and more balanced.

Another thing the super rich are guilty of is finding ways to avoid taxes completely, or paying far less as a percentage of their earnings than the rest of us. They always find all sorts of deductions in their business models that the average middle class worker will never had access to. And if they want to move money off shore, as they often do, even more reason to tax them a great deal for the honor of making those profits on our soil. Progressive tax transfer payments help to protect our currency so long as the use of any transfer is used responsibly, such as investing in education, food, or healthcare. This kind of transfer payment should not be seen as wasteful because in the grand scheme of things, it's actually an investment in the middle class, which is a far more rewarding place to put money than a handful of billionaires.

If increased taxation is balanced out with increasingly stricter controls over government debt at the same time, this would force politicians into a more accountable position. It would also force overgrown industries to expose their imbalances as they compete for their piece of the total economic pie. If the monetary policy were to shift to a system of finite money and finite resources, it would force smarter decisions toward what is truly most important for society as whole. But so long as we continue behind the smoke and mirrors of infinite math and postponed discipline, the reforms will never come, and the 1968 middle class will never return. Inside power will continue to have the upper hand as we all try to ice skate over the slippery waters of easy money ponzi schemes put on by the Fed.

Under the current state of affairs, it is impossible to build a governing model that limits debt because the Fed has created a system where money is constantly losing value. It makes them all feel good because it allows the numbers to keep growing, even if the real purchasing power behind those numbers are running in place on a mathematical treadmill. Because the Fed has created a very deep hole for us to crawl out of, the necessary transition is being made more and more difficult by the day. Higher interest rates, which are badly needed, are normally associated with austerity because all of the burdens of massive debt failure are often tossed over to the middle class to pay up. The only way to supplement this problem is to use a progressive tax system to get money flowing back to the people where value was stolen from in the first place.

MC4: Progressive taxation helps to increase competition among elites, which is important for getting the real cream to rise to the top. It also makes it harder for elites to unfairly abuse the system for their own interests.

The Cost: Analysts never accurately calculate the cost benefit of progressive taxation because they are unaware of gains it puts on the overall economy. The 1960s economy gives a clear idea how well it works— thanks to the 1950s progressive tax rates a decade earlier. The middle class gain could be 20% above today's current state if we could ever return to very high progressive rates on high income. We can't simply measure the transfer to understand the full value. The increase in competition among elites will add other exponential factors to the transfer that are typically omitted from the actual calculation.

It would also restore a great deal of morality to our government. The only moral government is one that answers first and foremost to its middle class. Our current generation has never known such a government.

FIVE

Negative Leverage

Some of you may die, but that is a sacrifice I am willing to make. Lord Farquaad of Shrek.

Corporations have been quite successful at turning the government into a better business bureau, which is actually not the most efficient way for a government to function. This is one of the avenues by which the elites have managed to inflate their value out of reach of the rest of us. Corporate nepotism with our government creates a shared waste in both the government and the corporations involved. And the first place to look for waste in any government is right near the center of the power structure—the military. The US military is bigger than all other militaries of the world combined. If you think our banking system is overgrown, that's nothing compared to our defense sector. Private sector defense manufacturers have the power and the incentive to sell the government far more war material than it needs. The severe lack of discipline in the defense industry has led to a lack of discipline in virtually everything else our government takes on. The restraint of power has been the hardest lesson for any world power to master, and the United States has certainly not been any exception.

The defense industry is well beyond what we actually need to defend ourselves. Their market niche is akin to a religion because they can get their customer (the government) to exploit patriotism in order to boost their profit motive. Having excessive military hardware on hand has made our government more violent than it should be. We have dropped so many bombs in poor parts of the world, it's simply beyond rational. The resulting environmental damage left behind by our modern weaponry is literally creating birth defects in our leftover war zones. Our own government studies show us that most of this aggression abroad has not made our country safer. But we continue down the same path anyway to the extreme pleasure of the defense industry.

Other industrialized countries, with more appropriately sized defense systems, are in far better financial condition, leaving their middle class with superior resources. If the United States fails to ever rein in our excessive spending on military ventures, we could eventually suffer the same financial fate as Russia. Sometimes a corrupt industry can only be stopped when the overall economic system finally goes broke, spending itself to death. Death by economic military excess has a long, painful past in the history of dying empires.

Our defense industry is a private industry tied to government purchasing, which is the sweetest type of business to be in. The incest between the military and our politicians is so extreme, it is virtually impossible for any elected official to speak out against the massive over-investment in defense spending. It's virtually unpatriotic to raise any major objections.

Probably the only politician to have ever uttered the full truth about this excessive use of American force was Ron Paul in the 2012 Republican Presidential primary. Most of his criticism of our military policy aligned perfectly with our own government's intelligence research. But Mr. Paul's criticism ultimately came across as incomprehensible to his peers. The mythical indoctrination imposed on the political structure by the defense industry's marketing department is fictional yet, both powerful and pervasive in political thought. The only real miracle to this story was the fact that a single politician finally said something that was actually factual about our international policy in a major political forum.

The ultimate beauty of the defense industry is that they can get the government to spend trillions of dollars without even putting the cost on our balance sheet. For some reason, we use Enron style accounting with wars, where the cost has been converted to an inert substance, like helium. The middle class began to decline in the 1970s, right after the massive, delayed, hidden spending in Vietnam began to set in. And the same result has occurred from Kuwait, Iraq, and Afghanistan. The cost secretly gets passed back to the American economy on a delayed timer, where politicians can find other scapegoats for the economic suffering at a future date.

The middle class loses a great deal of wealth from an overextended military, primarily because military spending does not produce a positive return on our investment. If our military were blatantly robbing material from other countries, the way England did a few centuries ago, then there could be a large return on the investment. It's obvious that our government's obsession with the Middle East is entirely connected to the oil resources there. But the money we spend on this obsession militarily does not calculate in any rational way to the overall oil market. The results are far more Orwellian since most of our military activity is primarily geared to simply use up vast amounts of ammunition. The only return we get back is mostly increased resentment from other parts of the world. Putting more of this wasted defense money back in the hands of the middle class economy would be highly leveraged wealth because money would be transferred from a system of negative leverage to a system of positive leverage.

Our military spending is reported to be around 4% of GDP, which is probably grossly underreported if you look at the full reach of military investment, intelligence, and research. But if we go along with that claim, then most other wealthy countries do just fine at 1% or 2% GDP on defense. Because we are a very wealthy country, spending just 1% or less of our GDP would still produce a massive military that any other country would be foolish to challenge. Politicians have heated debates, not on how much to cut military spending, but rather how much *growth* in spending to cut. We are nowhere near seeing the painful reality of our overextension. Ron Paul was correct in stating that this excessive power is well beyond what we can afford.

The middle class will need to think carefully about what these expensive ventures are costing us in terms of quality of life. Ironically, the two Presidents who gave us the clearest warnings about this danger of obsessive military power were both ex-military generals: Eisenhower and Washington. Their warnings have yet to be heeded. A hawkish attitude prevails today while our skyrocketing debts predict hard times ahead for the middle class if we fail to wake up from the madness.

Even our penitentiary system suffers from massive overbuilding as well. 25% of all prisoners in the world sit in American prisons. That's puts us nearly 500% above the world average for incarceration. The corporate market is slowly trying to increase its profits in this industry with the same kind of overreach as our military. Our crime rates are not necessarily any lower from all this extra effort. Somehow most other countries have managed to be just as safe as we are (if not safer), without locking up so many people.

The over-marketing of our insecurity is done for the purpose of overselling aggression. This affects how we treat people abroad, but it also affects how we treat people living among us. It's a boom-bust approach to life itself, and as a result, our middle class is getting sucked into both the booms and the busts of all the fear, paranoia, and aggression that get marketed to serve both our criminal justice system as well as our military. In a way, these two excesses are quite related, and both are very popular talking points for politicians.

The last thing any good democracy needs is a defense industry that's constantly looking ahead to market the next war. As military assets build up, you can rest assured our government will be on the lookout for the next opportunity to ignite massive quantities of munitions in a poor part of the world. Bombs and bullets need to be used in order to make room for new ones. Corporate bonus checks paid out in the defense industry depend on it. The ability to profit from war is a horribly immoral incentive to allow in any free market system. Any cursory tour of a defense industry trade shows will reveal that it has become a business no different than any other—in seek of market expansion, completely indifferent to the massive amount of violence they are selling. Now that we are able to destroy people and their cities in the manner of a video game, this has a dehumanizing effect on the violence that we create. War is able to stay toned down to a PG-13 level, so that it can be easily sold by our news media for public acceptance.

If you travel to a wealthy country that is not burdened with such heavy military spending, you will likely find a middle class *and* working class living a more comfortable, less stressful life. The cost of our last two wars is estimated to be as high as $6 trillion. If we spread that cost out over 15 years, that's about $400 billion per year, every year. Considering the results, this has to be one of the worst returns on an investment ever made. Those costs would have never been approved if they had been accurately estimated and proposed for a straight up or down vote prior to the war. It's an outrageous amount of money. Most American war efforts have been geared to last as long as the American public can tolerate. The industry learned with Vietnam that they can milk this thing a lot longer if they stop drafting soldiers and switch to an all volunteer military. That has greatly reduced the social pressure for any financial discipline to our absurdly expensive violence.

Reducing a massive military is one of the single hardest things for any empire to do. There are no instances in history where this was ever done voluntarily. It usually happens through economic failure, or public exhaustion of the violence. Bin Laden was able to spend a few million dollars to attack the United States. Presumably his aim was to get us to spend ourselves to death fighting back the way Russia did. He didn't exactly succeed, but getting us to drain out $6 trillion from our economy was overall a pretty amazing response ratio. Some of our violence was no doubt being pushed by certain international corporate interests trying to secure natural resources. But with each passing war we take on, it is looking more and more like an effort to simply use up as much military equipment as possible, for as long as possible, before the public finally can no longer afford the costs.

We fought this war on a credit card, and like all previous wars, the pain from the wasted money shows up in the following decade in the form of economic weakness. The payback has arrived in the form of lack of jobs and high unemployment. Our children are graduating from college with less opportunity. We also failed to increase our VA to take care of all the extra wounded soldiers. Since most of the funding was given over to corporate weapons manufacturers, little remains to help out the soldiers who did all the work and took all the risks.

$400 billion dollars a year for 15 years is a lot of money. That can help a lot of Americans here at home. That's about $4000 per family per year for nearly half a generation. Instead of investing in the middle class, we tried to convert some relatively medieval countries to a democracy instead. Was it really worth all that? Would you have rather received a lump sum payment of $60,000? That's what you paid already for a war, and it doesn't even include the normal cost of keeping a standing army in peace time. What could you do with an extra $60,000 in your pocket? Was all the international testosterone really worth all that?

For all the complaining about the Wall Street bail-outs, the military spending on war was actually far more expensive. The Fed bailout was partly just temporary leveraging rather than actual expenditures. At the peak of the bailout, they leveraged up to $12.8 trillion—about double the cost of our last 2 wars. But when you remove the temporary leveraging from the real net cost, the military spending in fact dwarfs our Wall Street bailout by over 500%. Most of the total cost of the bailout was in the billions of dollars, not trillions. So if you are incensed about the bailouts, you should be many times more offended by what the American people spent blowing up sand in the Middle East.

There is nothing less productive than violence. Ever since Russia's check on American power subsided (with their own bankruptcy from military excess), American power has become far more aggressive around the world, and far more expensive for our middle class. Our excessive use of power should not be viewed as a sign of power. It's a sign of severe corporate arrogance coupled with intense marketing of insecurity. We are reaching a point where we are fighting broke which is the kind of army Hitler had. While we struggle to survive the severe expenses, our peer countries are living far more comfortably, since they spend so much less than we do on their militaries.

If you look at the planning papers that are put out by the defense industry, you can literally look into the future of their war plans. Most of these wars do not happen as spontaneously as you think. Politicians will make them appear to be spontaneous, but the industry has a very good idea when and where they will be able to extract money in the future. They pretty much plan years in advance of places they have in mind for America to exert power. George Washington hoped we would never do this. Ron Paul has accurately said we cannot afford this. Dwight Eisenhower said we might never be able to stop it.

The defense industry makes broad assumptions that the world is completely depending on us to show our muscle. The suppliers both want and need our government to be a world police system. Their market growth is totally dependent on that goal. And the place they are looking now is Asia. They believe with the rise of power in Asia, our presence there is going to become increasingly important. But to the contrary, our presence is not wanted there, and as Asia grows more powerful, we will be playing with more fire as we keep making arrogant presumptions about what other countries really want from us.

If Americans don't start getting wise to this game, we are going to continue to be bled to death by machismo chess games. One can only hope that we might go back to a strong currency with very high interest rates in order to break the one industry that thinks it can get spend whatever it wants. If our government had to work in a solvent system, the real price of violence could be presented more accurately. When politicians start having to work with today's dollars, instead of future dollars, they would be forced to give the middle class a choice in how we use our wealth and power. At the moment, they think they can sell off your healthcare, education, and well being, so they can go set off bombs in a place you have never heard of. They think you won't notice. And from time to time, they will try to get you mad enough to go along with it because they know if you can get a taste for vengeance, you will forget about the money they are robbing from your children to finance it.

The accounting methods used to accomplish our massive financial excess in defense spending is far beyond anything Enron could have dreamed up. What is constantly overlooked is that the middle class gets hit far harder than anybody else from this abuse of power. Our forefathers worried about us becoming a military state because they knew the downhill spiral this leads to. Our middle class is a modern invention, but the financial catastrophe behind excessive military spending is as old as civilization.

MC5: Converting aggression money to more peaceful economic sectors will pay back triple the value, converting negative leverage into positive leverage.

The cost: A properly downsized military would boost the wealth of the middle class by 15%. Our war debts will keep our middle class in pain for another decade at minimum—longer if our country continues to look for more fights that we cannot afford.

Likewise, if the criminal justice system were brought down to the world norm, the poor would feel the most benefit with a 15% wealth improvement as well as an immeasurable increase in happiness.

SIX

Patented

Elites overvalue themselves by undervaluing the middle class.

Billionairism sees the world as an infinite field of weeds. Everybody gets to plant roots, drink water, and grow to the best of their ability. If a few manage to grow into trees, then good for them. There are no specified limits on how many people should be super rich versus middle class versus poor. The fact that most of us are mere weeds, and a few get to be trees, success of the few places no limitation on the rest of us. It's an open ended math model that is viewed in exact parallel with the infinite nature of progress, knowledge and discovery. There is no limit on how much can be discovered, there is no limit on what we can know, there is no limit on what we can invent, therefore, it stands to reason there is no limit to how much wealth any one individual can obtain. It's a guilt free system for the billionaire because it allows him to never see his wealth as a privilege, and most importantly, his success is never viewed as something that can possibly be of any danger to anybody else. Little wonder why the Koch brothers are so enamored with libertarian thinking—an Ayn Rand world without any reins whatsoever on individual success.

Economies are not open ended systems. Perhaps they could be if none of us had any needs for each other whatsoever. But we are not independent planets floating around in space. We are all consumers who are forced to drink from the same well. Our consumerism sets up the values of the trade mechanisms that cause goods and services to flow. It's a closed end system. And the fact that it's not infinite is the very reason why unfair advantages from excessive wealth *can* create disadvantages for others. An efficient economy should be creating a balance between production capacity and consumption capacity.

Economist Hernando de Soto has done a thorough analysis of the poor in order to understand what makes some countries poor while others are rich. He notes that even giant shanty towns around the world have internal economic structures that function at a very basic level. But they do so in what he refers to as the extralegal economy. Because they must live informally, without real government backed land ownership, access to banking credit, or insurance coverage, they live locked in a permanently inferior economic position compared to the wealthier legalized classes above them. When there is a giant gap between classes of people, you will find some sort of leveraging in the system that helps to form that separation. The growing gap between the middle class and the rich is also being caused by systematic advantages used for separation purposes.

The American economy is worth a certain amount of money—about $55 trillion at last count. That's a finite set of resources being controlled by a finite population. The Fed confuses the issue when they constantly inflate money because it makes assets and debt appear as though they can be infinite without any problem. But this is a mere magic trick that distorts reality. Our food, energy, and water resources are finite. Our population and property are specific. When we see something in the economy that seems financially outrageous, people tend to shake their head in disgust. Ambulance chasers abusing insurance claims, incompetent CEO's getting massive golden parachutes, or lawyers earning billions of dollars from class action law suits would all be well known examples. The lack of tort reform in this county is very expensive, and we are probably the most litigious society in the world. The rest of us pay a dear price for this because these excessive liabilities steal capacity from the economy. Your doctor bills are going to be a lot higher if they have to pay massive amounts of liability insurance to stay in business. The cost comes back to roost when bad economic policies continue to exist unrepaired.

Most of the leverage between the rich and middle class can be found in the corporate sector. The middle class, while very large in number, is not really an organized group. It's more like a series of highly disorganized individuals. The corporate sector is far more organized. They can easily out-lobby 100 million families about as easily as one family. Corporations can react faster and stronger to any threats to their wealth, whereas the middle class does not have any hired, dedicated, full time specialists, working for nice bonus checks to aggressively push their agenda. Corporations not only organize individually, but they also work in tandem, through highly organized industry groups, all setup to protect their markets by keeping a close eye on the government. This keeps them in a permanently leveraged position out of balance with the more helpless middle class consumer.

The corporate take or corporate share of the economic pie is hugely overvalued relative to the value of the middle class. This translates to the oversized paychecks that the corporate leadership collects. Many of our most powerful industries are vastly overgrown. This would normally be considered efficient if their growth was in proportion to need. But in too many cases their growth is actually hyper-efficient, causing overgrowth and overvaluation. This has the effect of putting more in the pockets of the seller while leaving a lot less in the pockets of the consumer. In other words, many corporations are doing their job too well. If the corporate side grows to be huge and powerful, and the middle class does not grow in tandem, with equal power, the result is a damaging imbalance and a clear sign of structural corruption. Our government has become blind to any sort of imbalance in the corporate world. There is zero awareness to this problem in economic circles because when dollar signs are involved, all everybody can see is success. America is not known for any ability to see proportionality.

The elites want you to believe that we are all in this together due to the fact that their corporations are filled with middle class employees. Their loss would effectively be our loss should we challenge their wealth model. But this is a convenient distortion of the truth. First of all, corporations are not the only employers in the marketplace. Small businesses and the government sector employee more people. Second of all, the corporate sector is not a very responsible employer if they create huge supply imbalances in the marketplace that rob the citizens of critical financial vitality. For the average middle class worker who might be an employee of an overgrown corporate sector, their job is a mirage to begin with should the excess ever be properly corrected to the optimum proportion of the whole.

These would normally be the accusations thrown at government. But corporate America is guiltier than government at forcing inefficiency and excess into the economy. It's a bit hard to blame our problems on government when corporate America is basically calling all the shots.

The specialists working in the various corporate arenas are not paid to see how small and efficient their industries should be. George Soros has written extensively about the corporate structure's inability to rein in control during a market bubble. As he puts it, participation in bubbles is literally mandatory in the corporate model, in virtually jingoistic fashion. The American corporate industry has an extreme talent for growing way beyond what is necessary, and our political system has an extreme talent for helping them get there. We live in a very obese country, with obese desire. Everybody wants a second dessert.

The best bubble for any elite power source is a permanent bubble that can last for multiple generations, if not centuries. When a particular consumer dogma is able to become endemic to the legal structure itself, it's a dream world for those privileged enough to pull off that kind of strategic stranglehold on the system. Once a bad system stays in place long enough, it becomes accepted as part of the culture, even if it's extremely unhealthy economically. Slavery went on for centuries as a way of life that was not to be questioned. Those who dared to imagine a slavery free world were considered wild eyed, liberal idealists. It was extremely profitable for a few, but obviously damaging to the whole. Forms of corporate entrenchment today enslave parts of our modern economy in ways that most people simply take for granted, even to the point to assuming it must be good.

It must be recognized that organizational excess is nothing new to civilization. Corporations were not the first to pull this off. This has been going on since the dawn of civilization. Excessive organizational growth is endemic to all civilizations. It's our human nature, and it's as old as religion. Corporate power is a mere offshoot of previous systems that all accomplished the same overreach. What we have yet to find in large societies are systems that will actually seek out proper balance. Economies are not only like ecosystems, we should start viewing them exactly like ecosystems because they actually serve all living things. Healthy ecosystems do not seek maximum growth. Healthy ecosystems seek out maximum *balance*, for long term stability.

Probably the oldest place to find systematic excess would be in the agricultural industry. With food being so tied to our biology, it is the easiest place to exploit human emotion with political policy. And because starvation was more common in the past than now, it stands to reason why governments would go to extremes to push various agricultural agendas beyond their reasonable balance. The American food production system is heavily dominated by meat, dairy, sugar, corn and wheat. And to the casual eye, these would appear to be natural results of dietary and cultural selection. [Asia's culture is dominated by rice instead of wheat, and soy instead of diary. Different parts of the world have focused on their own specific food groups to overexploit.] But our focusing of assets to these restricted groups has produced damaging excess. The average American consumes far more protein than what is actually healthy as a percentage of our diet. Our meat industry, with the financial backing of our government, has overgrown way beyond what we need, and way beyond what any other country in the world has done. We suffer from many degenerative diseases that excessive amounts of animal protein help to create (such as osteoporosis). It's also very wasteful to our water resources, and damaging to the environment. Too much corn is produced, largely to help support the meat industry. And wheat is overly dominant as a food source, displacing a lot of other grain options from our diet. Government policy has evolved over the years to reinforce these lopsided imbalances to very select industries. This overgrowth has crowded out many other foods that we need.

Our ancient ancestors used to consume some 200 to 300 different food sources in their diet. That's the kind of diet diversity our bodies evolved with over thousands of years. Today's modern American lives off of less than 50 to 60 primary food sources. Not only is this unhealthy for our bodies, it is also not sustainable to our ecosystem, increasing the need for pesticides.

Our corporate system has pushed this reduction in diversity in an effort to maximize profit and serve the large scale interests of the fast food industry. It has been referred to as the mono-culture incentive, encouraged by typical corporate business models seeking to optimize profit. The long term benefit to our species using this corporate food model is very unhealthy, increasing our healthcare cost, increasing the rates of degenerative disease, and lowering our quality of life. A more responsible government policy would be one that tries to increase food diversity, which would be better for our health, better for the environment, and reduce the need for expensive pesticides and chemicals.

Sugar has long been highly protected by the government, funneling billions of dollars to a small handful of sugar farmers in order to protect them from much cheaper international competition. But the real beneficiary is the heavily subsidized corn industry, which gets to sell its corn sweetener to American food manufacturers as the primary sweetener of choice, at an artificially low price. Americans consume over 150 pounds of sugar per year. A century ago, Americans only consumed about 12 pounds per year. Science is slowly starting to realize that our excessive sugar intake might be one of the most dangerous and damaging habits we have. With one of the highest obesity rates in the world, we certainly have the results to show for it.

Our government never gives much thought to what kind of food supply would be in the best interest of its population. Instead, it has listened to the marketing desires of the agribusiness industry which has promoted huge imbalances in our farming system for their personal profit. Instead of using nutritional education to think about what we *should* be eating, our senses are exploited by habit, convenience, addiction, and heavy advertizing to make us feel better about treating ourselves so poorly. This is a leveraging process that takes money from the middle class without returning any increased value. If the entire world lived off the American diet, the world's entire food supply would completely collapse immediately. It's simply not sustainable on any global scale.

But wait, it gets worse, a lot worse. Genetic engineering has taken over the interests of major agriculture corporations because it is a clear path to patents, which mean super high profits for an industry that used to be very dull, boring, and low margin. But genetics has created a very new mindset because it is providing corporations a pathway to privatize and outright own Mother Nature. The economic gains for them are massive, while the economic losses to the masses can be equally extraordinary. We have survived for thousands of years using cheap, natural seeds, but our patent system is inducing corporate agribusiness to modify the structure of seeds so that they can own them like an invention, and charge a lot more money for us to grow our food. These same corporations have also been quietly trying to eliminate natural seeds from the marketplace, buying up old seed warehouses and disposing of the natural product so that only private, expensive, patented product can be purchased.

The FDA has been a proud assistant to this abusive industry, allowing our food supply to be reengineered without any requirement for special labels. The consumer is kept in the dark about which foods are being modified, giving them no say in the matter. It's basically impossible now to purchase a russet potato that does not have 1% beetle pesticide in it. Our fast food chains wanted to serve the exact same French fry all over the world. The corporate desire to provide only one species of potato creates an imbalance with Mother Nature which could easily cause a potato famine like Ireland had. The ancient Peruvians never had a potato famine because they farmed over 200 different types of potatoes in a diverse, rich, sustainable agricultural system. The corporate food industry is trying to solve the problem with unhealthy chemicals engineered into our food. The Peruvians solved the problem thousands of years ago, simply by eating a more diverse diet. Our economic patent model does not encourage improvement. Their only problem is there's no big money to be made with any natural approach. There is no patent to be had from "natural." The very dull business of growing food is now a very "exciting" business called patented, high profit, GMO farming. The leveraging of profit is now moving into the food industry using the same abusive economic model developed by drug companies in previous decades.

Europe has always been a step ahead of us in this regard, taking their food quality more seriously, and their more diverse, more eco-friendly farming system is better protected. The American corporate agriculture system has been running most farmers out of business for the past 50 years, leaving only giant agribusiness corporations in charge. They try really hard to twist the arm of Europe to let them do the same unhealthy processes over there. The pressure to adopt our inferior model is constant and ongoing. Corporations never stop trying to expand. They can be relentless until they finally get their way.

Our healthcare system is far more expensive than any other system in the world—nearly twice the price per citizen as the second most costly system

(Switzerland). And despite our super high per capita spending, that money is not arriving at the point of healthcare delivery. There are so many highly organized forces who have managed to take a big piece of the pie, there is less and less available at the receiving end for the average American patient, or even for the well intentioned doctor.

We are not delivering the best healthcare in the world despite spending the most money in the world. Could there be any better example of middle class robbery? All other industrialized countries have us beat on quality in almost all medical specialties. The most efficient thing about the American health care system is the amount of money it is able to deliver to the private insurance industry and pharmaceutical giants. If there is one thing we do really well, is protect the corporations who serve the system. But the clear loser here is our middle class.

Economic dogma creates a tremendous problem with healthcare. The classic supply-demand curve gets a bit out of whack when you get a person's health involved. In decisions of life or death, the so called free market demand curve goes through the roof, and the corporate world has wisely exploited that fear for absurd profit. When a person's life is at stake, he cannot provide a specific price tag to his survival. We cannot hold auctions in the ICU, but our system has a way of doing just that in countless indirect ways. The United States is truly unique and alone in the world for thinking it can apply so much free market profiteering to such a critical public need.

The government provides tremendous economic protection to allow the pharmaceutical industry to overvalue its products. If you look at the real cost of drug ingredients relative to the prices they can charge, the profit ratio is higher than anything else mankind has ever produced. The markup in many cases is several thousand percent per pill. And on the world market, the United States is routinely the highest bidder on nearly every kind of pharmaceutical product out there. Our government oddly goes out of its way to maximize the profits of the drug company, with little regard for what this is doing on the consumer side.

The regulation methodology of the entire pharmaceutical industry is fairly corrupt. The FDA has devised a regulatory system where major drug companies are literally allowed to police themselves. Furthermore, the peer review scientific research system is highly dominated by corporate financing, where corruption is often uncovered in the reporting of data. Corporations are not going to invest millions of dollars in a study unless they are fairly certain it will support their investment. Objective, honest, scientific analysis does not mix real well with free market capitalism. Honesty is not always the best friend of profit.

As science gets more sophisticated and more microscopic, it gets easier for participants to tell little white lies about what they are selling. Because of the profit motive for patents, anything that cannot be patented, like older drugs, vitamins, herbs, nutrition, and healthy living, are not well financed or studied much because there's no big money to be gained there. Pharmaceutical companies have a very narrow profit focus that is heavily trained on patented profit incentives. The result is an American population that is heavily drugged, overcharged, and not so healthy.

Drug companies figured out a long time ago that treating a disease is far more profitable than curing one. You almost never hear the word *cure* anymore, as it has been virtually eliminated from the medical lexicon. The *treatment* of disease is the primary goal because that's the most profitable incentive. If you need a drug for the rest of your life, that will produce far more profit than taking a temporary dose. Even vaccines are moving in this direction. Our healthcare system has become a drug *treatment* system. Without a major change to these misplaced incentives, the cost will always be excessive.

For those rare few who have studied the overall effectiveness of the pharmaceutical industry versus other alternatives, some have estimated that over 50% of all drugs on the market may not be the patient's best option to better health, or the most economical pathway to better health. Clearly, we have many miraculous drugs being used for great good, but what is not well studied is all of the unpatented solutions that might work better, safer, or cheaper than what is typically marketed. The legal framework behind the patent system intentionally eliminates *all* other options from the academic range of consideration. Our intellectual capacity is heavily overbalanced to the best patent, rather than the best human need. It's a sad economic defect that is too complex for most to comprehend.

A well known health care critic—Gary Null—provided a telling example back in the 90s concerning the complexity of misplaced incentives in the pharmaceutical industry. [I will retell the story, stripping out the names of the corporations and products involved since the actual outcome is not really relevant to the point at hand.] For years our ERs used a $200 drug, I will refer to as Drug A, to treat heart attack victims (acute myocardial infarction). Then a leading drug company spent millions of dollars to do a comparative study of Drug A to their new drug I will refer to as Drug B, which sold for $2200 per dose. The efficacy difference between the two drugs was extremely small, less than a 1%; nevertheless, we had a company willing to spend a ton of money prove out their very slim margin of victory to sell a much more expensive product. At the same time, some European countries were using intravenous magnesium for the same purpose, which some would argue was just as effective, with fewer side effects than both of the patented drug options. The magnesium sold for only $5 or $10 a dose. Nobody can patent magnesium which is why it is so dirt cheap. And because it cannot be patented, it cannot even be considered for treatment in America because technically it is not a drug. It takes millions of dollars to classify something as a "drug" in this country. Our legal incentives conveniently exclude all options from consideration except for the most expensive, patented options.

In the end, we have to trust the peer review system to figure out which medical treatments really work best. But this particular example helps to illustrate how our patent system is literally destroying everything in its path with excessive valuation and excessive power. We have created a model where many Americans are starting to doubt the integrity of our peer review system because so much money is at stake in the outcome of privately funded studies. And worst of all, our very lopsided incentive system is preventing a massive world of natural options from ever competing against the privatized alternative. When a drug company explores a distant jungle to hopefully discover a new miracle herb that might provide the next miracle cure, they are not looking to use that herb in their medicine. That would not be profitable. They are looking for the next herb that they can synthesize, modify, patent and own. Then and only then does it make economic sense. Mother Nature is only useful to the extent that our corporations can find a way to take private ownership of her secrets for escalated monopolized profits.

Drug companies are known for making super tiny changes to their most popular drugs right before their patent expires, simply to keep them out of the cheaper generic market. The entire existence of the patent industry is taken for granted as a good thing, simply because nearly all of corporate America is on the take, making vast fortunes from this *exception* to free market capitalism. But in reality, they are making their fortunes based on monopoly power and a legalized pardon from real competition. They complain that this leveraged profit is necessary for them to fund expensive discoveries. But it also works in reverse. This incredible gift induces them to seek out the most expensive solutions possible, rather than the most economical, or even the safest, healthiest, or most natural.

The vaccine industry is also getting corrupted by this incentive. Drug companies have now figured out to not only patent the vaccine, but also their manufacturing process. Vaccine makers have filed thousands of patents since the 90s to convert their industry into a much more expensive, higher profit business. And now it's getting harder and harder for people to afford vaccines. On top of that, vaccine makers are protected by a special vaccine court system where the government will assume all liability on their behalf. All of these little adjustments that corporations keep making to refine their business model helps to make the entire industry increasingly expensive and less efficient.

The patent is the single biggest cause of wealth disparity in the free market. It's ironic that free market capitalism is preached as the savior of mankind, to be worshipped and respected by all. But the one thing in our system that every corporation wants to dominate is the patent system, which is the one tool designed to actually bypass free market capitalism. Who wouldn't want monopoly protection in a competitive market? Its origins are innocent enough, but when corporations put their mind to something useful, they will squeeze it beyond recognition to get all the money they can. Just as lawyers abuse law suits and liability, both corporations and lawyers abuse patent incentives for leveraged profit.

The excess in patent law has virtually wrecked our technology sector. Technology companies now spend a lot of their resources trying to buy up additional patents primarily for lawsuit protection. It has gotten so bad that even law firms are starting to buy technology patents themselves, simply so they can go blackmail real technology companies into payoffs. Where an average middle class inventor might have one or two patents in their lifetime, corporations file thousands of patents every single year, primarily for the purpose of trying to dominate intellectual real estate. It has become a money grab as well as a courtroom grab. It has reached the level of absurdity that is very damaging to our middle class.

Until we factor in the tremendous damage caused by patents, the problems we face will remain mysterious for years to come. This should give us great pause as to exactly why we have patents in the first place, and for what purpose are they really serving. There is a vast part of our ecosystem that cannot be patented, yet has tremendous solutions to offer. But all of our subsidies and research are heavily focused on private, proprietary, patented ownership. There is no balance to our intellectual, creative exploration because our economic system is over-rewarding a very narrow spectrum. The vast overgrowth of particular industries and their proprietary products is sucking money away from the rest of the population. It helps create vast wealth gaps because the leverage is unreasonable. This is not free market capitalism. This is systematic competition elimination at the corporate level. The more they perfect and improve this protection, they more imbalanced the wealth model will get.

An honest system should be rewarding brains, but not over-rewarding intellectual ownership. The length of patent protection is in severe need of reduction and constraint. The bar needs to be raised on what can be patented because at this time, the flood gates are still open, and the number of patents flowing in is creating vast damage to our overall creative and intellectual marketplace. The fact that our government sits by acting helpless to correct these huge imbalances in our legal framework is akin to allowing counterfeiting of our currency. Corporations have gotten smarter while the politicians they pay off have conveniently gotten dumber. Sadly, we need a more intelligent political class that can comprehend these abuses, but thanks to our incumbency protection, our politicians are not in need of intellectual development to keep their job.

Whenever we find a way to let the middle class break through these elitist barriers, the excessive profits and excessive salaries would drop very quickly to a normalized level. Most wealth gaps in any economic system exist due to legalized barriers that limit access while leveraging the profit to fewer players. The patent is the secret tool very quietly causing most of the damage.

MC6: Patent law is in severe need of restructuring. It's the single biggest contributor to overgrowth in the corporate sector.

The Cost: If healthcare were reformed to something closer to what every other industrialized country in the world is doing, middle class wealth would increase by 20%. But digging deeper, real patent reform could eliminate the wealth gap between the rich and the middle class by as much as 50%, if not more. It would help our food supply and health care system normalize, which in turn, would help improve our health, environment, diet, food affordability, and quality of life. Both our food and our healthcare would be more affordable in a far less patented world. You would also see a reversal in agriculture, where we could gain back all the middle class farmers that have been displaced by corporate agri-business since the 1960s.

SEVEN

Proportionality

Tombstone: Homo Sapiens
evolved: 98,219 BC, died: 2211 AD.
Sorry we couldn't save the planet from global warming,
but it wasn't economically feasible.

Now, more than ever, we need to fix more than the just the middle class. We need to fix problems with our planet. We are suffering from incompetent elites who are not willing to allow our best and brightest scientists to properly protect our entire planet from harm. The global warming issue is getting very serious very fast, and time is running out to do something about it. Climate scientists have been shocked and surprised at how corrupt their science has become. Had they known more about other branches of the scientific industry they would not be so surprised. They were simply isolated from the corruption until they came upon a problem that actually posed a real threat to corporate power—specifically the very powerful fossil fuels industry. The moment they brought this problem into the limelight, the giant corporate propaganda machine began to focus all of its corrupt tools in the direction of the unwanted message in order to denigrate truth and confuse the population as much as possible.

Our era of corporate protectionism is creating an incompetent, crony, corrupt elite. Until we fix the misplaced incentives in this economy we could be in a real mess simply because we are too corrupt to behave rationally or honestly to very basic human challenges. We have become a macrocosm of what we witnessed decades ago when the tobacco industry remained in constant denial about the dangers of smoking. We suffer from economic denial at multiple levels. Fixing the middle class should help fix global warming because both rely heavily on overcoming elite denial with intellectual fact.

We need to empower as many people as possible not only to restore our middle class, but to increase our intellectual capacity for solving serious issues. The middle class requires an intelligent, honest, transparent world to thrive in. We are the A-team America needs to move forward. Corrupt elites have become the main obstacle to open discourse. There is important work to be done and we need to get started *yesterday*. We have a debt to pay to our planet as well as our children.

If we shift more capital away from the most advantaged, and move it over to middle class needs, such as healthy food, clean water, cheap education, cheap healthcare, and CO_2 reduction, the payback from the middle class will be far superior to anything corporate insiders have to offer.

There are some fundamental belief systems that elites heavily depend on for imbalanced valuation and excessive control. Ultimately, these issues are why the middle class is getting so small and weak. These belief systems are part of American elitism and are used to form official policy for reinforced control.

Elitist dogma is primarily focused on just one thing—the privatization of everything. Cheap money, free trade, exclusive patents, less taxes, and less government are all part of the dogma. Ultimately, these are not competition *increasing* factors, but competition *decreasing* factors, that focus power to the few.

Billionairism (Elite Dogma):
- Less government & less regulation.
- Less taxation or flat tax rates.
- More patents and exclusive propriety.
- Low interest rates.
- Weak currency.
- Free (corporate) trade.
- Maximum public debt

There are no independent thinkers left to protect the one thing that is missing from this entire list of motivations: balance and proportion. *Transparency International* is an organization that was founded on the basic principle that honesty, transparency, and competence are at the very heart of an open and free society. Each year, they create a ratings list of every country in the world, measuring their ability to be honest and transparent. Each year that they update the survey, the United States never ranks in the top 10. We are typically around 16th place in the world. At the top of the list are mostly Scandinavian countries, well known for their honest business practices and transparent government systems. Everything the Scandinavians are doing flies in the face of American dogma, a dogma that believes government is inherently bad, dishonest, and inefficient. Scandinavian governments tend to have enormous control, are somewhat socialist, and their middle class tends to be well protected. They are living proof that government *can* be honest. Their success stands as a constant reminder that Reagan's view of government was dead wrong. Government *is* necessary, and it is good, so long as the effort is put in to keep it honest. It is no better and no worse than the citizens and companies it governs. It's not separate from us.

The heart of any successful system is one of competence and control of the overall asset balance of the country. Most of the more transparent countries view their middle class as a critical asset, so they put a lot of effort in to protecting it. The American model sees the middle class as a source of exploitation. Elites have never feared the middle class could ever disappear. Our existence has always been taken for granted as a simple byproduct of *their* success. *Balance* is not even part of the American vocabulary. We seem to live and die by our *all or nothing* approach to everything.

The American middle class will need to understand that a class war *is* underway. It has been going on since 1968, and as Warren Buffet said, his side is definitely *not* losing. The masses will need to develop a new skepticism about the current state of affairs in order to better embarrass the elites who have taken so much power. The *99% Occupy Wall Street* movement was probably the very first step, where ordinary activists put a spotlight directly in the eyes of excessive wealth. While the elites did a pretty effective job of discrediting the protestors with their usual propaganda tricks, this was definitely a wake-up call that put elites back on their heels.

The only real tools we have to combat imbalances are the benign amoral tools of the marketplace. We have a bubble in elite valuation that needs to pop. We can go after it with strong currency. Part of our currency reform, however, needs to include patent reform (the secret currency of super-wealth). The other easy tool is progressive taxation. That's the easiest shortcut to correcting social valuation imbalances. But it will be important to use these taxes for the right things because all popping bubbles can hurt the middle class citizens who are employed *within* these bubbles. Taxes are supposed to be a transfer of wealth to the poor or the middle class. If left unchecked, it could easily turn into a transfer back to the elite.

If the middle class is ever going to reform our own elites, there will need to be a plan in place that understands the critical variables. Restoring the middle class means restoring proper economic balance so our elite class can function more competently, honestly, and in better harmony with the rest of us:

Elite Reform:
- Transparent, skeptical government.
- Progressive taxation.
- Severe limits on patented propriety.
- Government control of critical services.
- Strong currency.
- Steady, moderate interest rates.
- Limited debt and limited liquidity.
- Appropriate middle class trade protection.
- Strong government based research.
- Limited banking and financialization.

We need a government smart enough to understand its role as a defender of not only the middle class, but also our education system. That also includes a need for a robust, government supported, academic research system that can remain free from the financial bias and control of the corporate sector. The scientific peer review system, in conjunction with the education system, needs to be government protected. There needs to be research done on solutions that do not fall within the patent profit model because unpatented solutions hold great promise for increased social prosperity. Because of excess in our patent system, millions of cheap solutions remain neglected from consideration. There is a serious need for our government to develop a broad search for the truth, rather than obsessing over alignment with elite profit motives, or the next big patented product. The government needs to be researching unpopular topics as well as the most serious challenges. We need a third party approach as only a government can provide. In a world full of corporate funded think tanks, we are missing the most vital of all think tanks—the government—where transparent, independent thinking can be fostered. It can be the least corruptible source of information, if we ever decide to take on Scandinavian competence to make it so.

We are faced with some very serious problems that are not being addressed because our distorted system is starting to not even listen to scientists or educated people anymore. We don't have another half century to restore honesty, respect and fair competition to the market. We need to quickly devise a system similar to the patent system that will incentivize the corporate world to pursue CO_2 reduction. If there is one area where excessive profit could be tolerable, planet protection sounds like a more reasonable justification.

In order to maintain a more balanced, sustainable world, there are some critical industries that we need to keep more restrained and boring. It's not that they should never innovate anything, but we have to make sure the incentives to innovate are not based on trying to artificially overgrow the industry into disproportionate positions that can hurt the rest of the economy. There is no reason why these businesses should be led by billionaires or highly overpaid elites:

- Education
- Agriculture and water
- Defense
- Healthcare
- Banking

When these industries get too big, too patent heavy, too privatized, or too ambitious, they can cause a lot more bad than good, and waste middle class money by the trainload. If these businesses are well run and well proportioned to their need, they should be safe, modest, and productive—you know, like the middle class. And that would be refreshing.

MC7: Basic necessities like food, water, healthcare, defense, banking and education should be kept away from privatization or excessive profit. We've had enough excitement in these areas for one century.

The Cost: Our sanity. Maybe even our survival.

0% for the Middle Class

0%

www.ingramcontent.com/pod-product-compliance
Lightning Source LLC
Chambersburg PA
CBHW021409170526
45164CB00002B/573